Siren's Atlas

AN OCEAN OF GRANNY SQUARES TO CROCHET

SHELLEY HUSBAND

UK TERMS EDITION

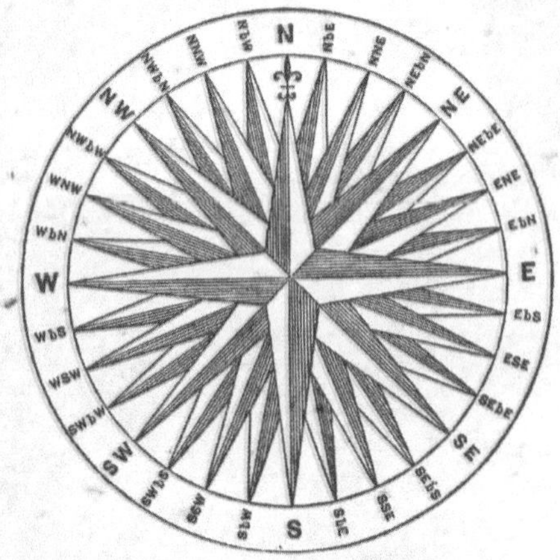

Charts made by Amy Gunderson

Email: kinglouiespizza@gmail.com
Ravelry ID: AmyGunderson

Graphic Design by Michelle Lorimer

Email: hello@michellelorimer.com

Project Photography by Jo O'Keefe

Email: jookeefe@hotmail.com
Instagram: missfarmerjojo

Other Photography by Shelley Husband

Technical Editing by SiewBee Pond

Email: essbee1995@yahoo.com

First edition 2019

Published by Shelley Husband
PO Box 11
Narrawong VIC 3285
Australia
www.spincushions.com

0822

Contents

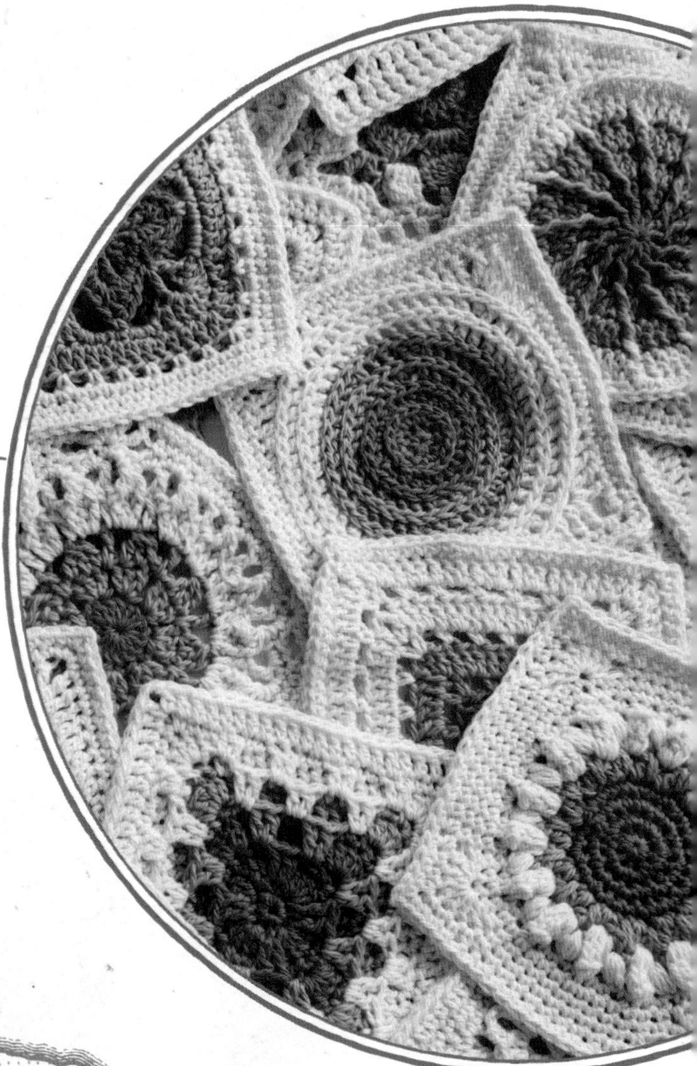

Welcome to Siren's Atlas

A journey through the oceans and seas of the world in crochet

I love nothing more than sitting down with my hook and some yarn to design new granny squares. It makes my heart and brain sing! In this book you will find sixty-four granny square patterns. All are named after seas, oceans and large bodies of water around the world.

Siren's Atlas was born from my need to create. I designed fifty-two of the squares in 2016, one each week and then published all the patterns digitally once a week in 2017. I have always wanted to compile the collection into print and so this Siren's Atlas book was born. Of course, I took the opportunity to design twelve more squares to add to the collection. Having sixty-four squares means you will have a sampler blanket of eight squares by eight squares should you choose to make them all.

So why "Siren's Atlas"? Well, as my colours were inspired by my daily view of the ocean, I wanted a sea theme, hence, naming all the squares after oceans and seas. Over the last few years, some of the fiction books I have read have been based on Greek mythology and so I came up with the idea of a Siren, swimming the waters of the world in search of her next victim. Surely, she would need a map of some sort? I also love old world maps – the really old ones before the entire world had been mapped, where parts were made up and it was assumed monsters roamed the oceans. The maps in this book showing the locations of the bodies of water are a homage to those old world maps.

The original Sirens, so the story goes, were companions to Persephone, the daughter of Zeus and Demeter who was abducted by Hades to become Queen of the Underworld. As a punishment for allowing Persephone to be taken, the maidens were transformed into harpy-like creatures, half bird, half women. They appeared to be beautiful while singing their Siren song, extolling the pleasures of the underworld. Upon succumbing to the Sirens' song, the victims saw the grotesque creatures for what they really were and became a feast for the Sirens. Over the years, these bird-women of myth have transformed into the highly sanitised, beautiful fish women we know as mermaids.

It was said that if a sailor could resist the Sirens' song, the Sirens would perish. In the tale of Odysseus, thanks to the prophetess Circe, Odysseus knew of this and came up with a plan to safely pass by the isle of the Sirens. He had his crew's ears blocked with wax so they would be safe, but he wished to hear the beauty of the Sirens' song. He ordered his crew to tie him to the mast and not give in to his pleas to be released should he be tempted. He was, yet his crew held firm and did not untie him and so they all passed safely and the Sirens perished.

My fiction for this book is that a single Siren was not there at the time and now roams the seas alone, seeking sailors to lure to their doom. And on that cheery note, let's get started on the crochet.

xx Shelley

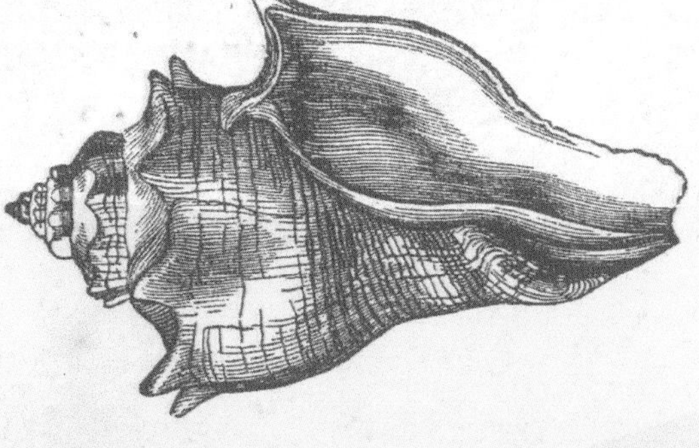

Before you start

What you need to have

Yarn and hook needs

All patterns in this book measure 15 centimetres/6 inches square when made with 8 ply/DK/light worsted cotton yarn and a 4.5 mm hook, if your tension is average. A small difference in size will not matter unless you are using patterns from this book to match with patterns from other sources. Your end result (blanket, bag, cushion, scarf) could turn out to be a little larger or smaller, but unless you are making garments, it does not matter.

The amount of yarn needed for each colour for each square is listed in the Yarn Information section on page 86.

You can of course use any yarn and hook combination. As long as you use the same hook and yarn throughout, your squares will work out to be approximately the same size.

As a crocheter with some experience, you will know how to deal with small differences in size, for example blocking to size, altering the last round of the pattern to use smaller or larger stitches, adding an extra round of double crochet to increase the size, or using a different hook size.

Blocking tools

If you have never blocked before, it really is a game changer once you try it. A lot of the squares in this book need blocking to make them sing. I do it very simply by pinning my squares out on a foam mat and shooting them with steam from my iron. Once they are dry and cool, you are all done. Joining the squares will help keep the squares nice and square, but blocking first is still recommended. It really opens out any lacy sections.

What you need to know

Skills

You need to know the most common crochet stitches. Plus, you need to be able to read a written pattern and/or chart and trust that it will work. Often in this book, the pattern will not become clear, or in some cases, flat and square, until the last couple of rounds. I let my design mind run wild when coming up with these patterns. There may be new stitch and technique combinations you have not seen before, but they are all based on the most common stitches and all are fully explained in the Glossary on page 84. The Glossary also shows all chart symbols.

Options

With crochet, there are standard, traditional ways to do things and more often than not the patterns in this book are written that way. However, there are instances when new or different techniques can be used to give a better result.

How to begin a square

I have noted in each pattern the way I feel is best for each individual pattern, but you can use your preferred method.

Starting chain alternative

The traditional way to begin a round of crochet is to start with a number of chain stitches that generally take the place of the first stitch. For example, if a treble crochet stitch is needed at the start of a round, it is traditional to chain 3 to take the place of the first stitch. This matches the height of a treble stitch and you are at the right place to begin the next stitch i.e. from the top down.

This starting chain can really stand out as different from other stitches when worked in the round, so to make that first stitch blend in I make a false stitch instead. Go to my YouTube Channel to see how it is done.

How to read the patterns and charts

All patterns are in written and charted format. Some patterns have many layers worked into, behind and on top of other rounds making them difficult to depict in chart form which is why some have been split into more than one chart. In some cases it is best to use both the written and charted pattern to be clear about how to work the stitches.

Where rounds end and begin in my patterns

For a seamless look, my patterns use a technique borrowed from doily patterns. A lot of doily patterns are made with long chain loops with a single stitch worked into the middle of those long chain loops in the next round. To avoid the need to slip stitch many times to reach the centre of a long chain loop, which would create a much thicker section that would stand out, these patterns are joined with a stitch. For example, if there was a round of 7-chain loops, the last 7-chain loop may be created by chaining 3 then joining with a double treble crochet.

This places your hook as if it is in the middle of the 7-chain loop, in the right place to make a stitch for the next round. The double treble pretends to be the second half of the 7-chain loop.

I use this methodology when designing my squares. In the case of a square with 2-chain corner spaces, the round will end with the instruction to chain 1 and join with a double crochet. That double crochet takes the place of the second chain and places your hook at exactly the right spot to begin the next round, with no need to slip stitch or work backwards. Depending on the pattern, you may be instructed to work a stitch over that joining stitch. Treat the joining stitch as the second chain of the 2-chain corner space and work over it as if it were a chain loop.

If the corners of the pattern are longer chain loops, the final number of chains to be worked and the joining stitch will be different. For example, if a round has corners of 4-chain spaces, it may end with chain 1, join with a treble crochet. A round with 3-chain spaces may end with chain 1, join with a half treble crochet.

How to read the written patterns

Here is an excerpt from a pattern:

R1: ch3 (stch), 2tr, *ch2, 3tr*, rep from * to * 2x, ch1, join with dc to 3rd ch of stch. {12 sts, 4 2-ch sps}

R2: dc over joining dc, *dc in next 3 sts**, (dc, ch2, dc) in 2-ch sp*, rep from * to * 2x and * to ** 1x, dc in same sp as first st, ch1, join with dc to first st. {5 sts on each side; 4 2-ch cnr sps}

R3: ch3 (stch), tr over joining dc, *2x [tr in next st, ch1, skip 1 st], tr in next st**, (2tr, ch2, 2tr)*, rep from * to * 2x and * to ** 1x, 2tr in same sp as first sts, ch1, join with dc to 3rd ch of stch. {7 sts, 2 1-ch sps on each side; 4 2-ch cnr sps}

Here is how to read it:

At the start of a round, I tell you how to begin, then you will see an asterisk. This single asterisk indicates the beginning of a repeat. Ignore it and keep working, following the instructions until you get to "rep". That is your cue to go back to the first single asterisk and repeat the stitches after it, as instructed. After the repeats are done, I tell you how to finish off the round.

The instructions between a single asterisk and the double asterisks equal one side only. The instructions between the double asterisks and single asterisk equal one corner. So that means the instructions between the first and last single asterisks equal one side and the following corner. This is true of a square pattern but it also works for sections of patterns that begin as other shapes.

In those cases, the instructions between the single asterisks are a full pattern repeat and those from the single asterisk to the double asterisks are a partial repeat.

Brackets

(xxxxx) are stitches and/or chain spaces that are either to be all worked in the one stitch or space as indicated, or a set of stitches and/or chain spaces to be skipped.

[xxxx] indicate a small set of stitches and/or chain spaces to be repeated within a pattern repeat. These brackets will be preceded with a number and x to indicate how many times to work the small repeat. E.g. 2x [xxxxxx] means to work the [stitches and/or chain spaces] twice.

{xxxx} contain the stitch count for each round. The stitch count states how many stitches are along each side between the corners and describe the corners. If the pattern begins as a shape with no corners, then it describes how many stitches in total make up that round.

NOTE: If there are a number of chain stitches at the start of a round not followed by (stch) they are not counted in the stitch counts. These are not a starting chain, but rather an aid to getting your hook to the right place to begin the round and will be invisible once the round is complete. Slip stitches to join rounds are also not counted in the stitch counts. However, if they are used in a pattern repeat, slip stitches are included in the stitch counts.

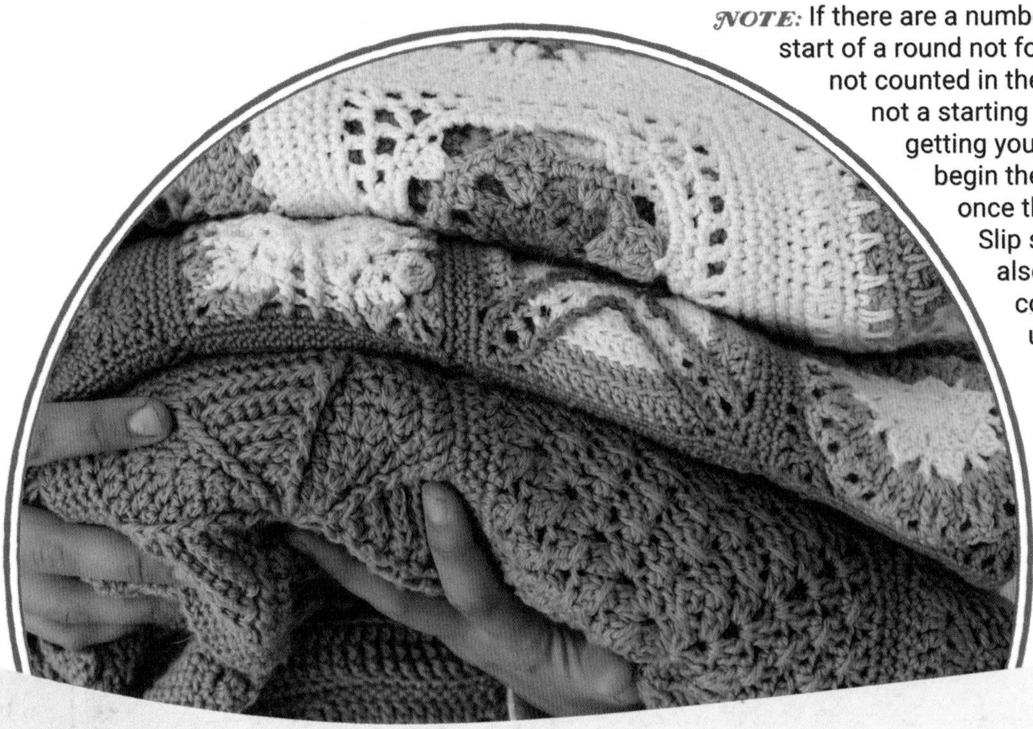

A word about stitch counts

Most of the sixty-four patterns in this book have a final stitch count along the sides of 21 or 23 stitches. The rest range from 19 to 25 stitches.

It is easy to deal with this difference if you join your squares by crocheting them together as I do. If the stitch counts are different, simply use a stitch on the shorter square twice while using new stitches on the longer square as you join. This can be repeated as many times as needed. Spread the double stitches out a little so they are not all together.

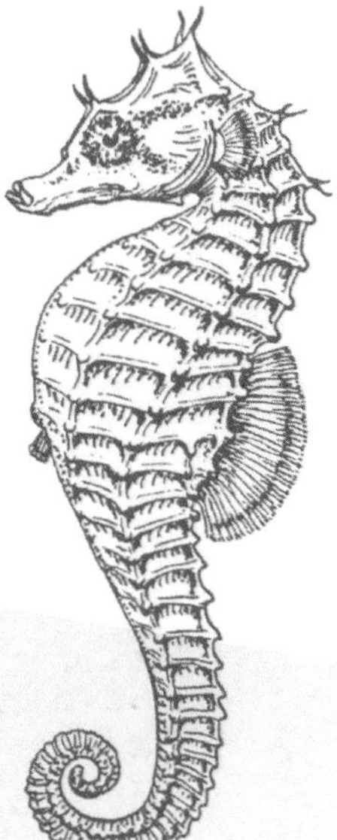

What you can make

Granny squares are not just for blankets. You can make cushions, scarves, bags, garments – the only limit is your imagination.

Blue Sampler Blanket; 155 x 170 cm; Pages 4, 11, 87
Yarn: Bendigo Woollen Mills 8 ply cotton
Colour: Sky
Hook: 4.5 mm
Layout: 10 x 11 squares
Squares used: all patterns x 1, 46 patterns x 2

Mini Sampler Blanket; 90 x 90 cm; Pages 7, 11
Yarn: Bendigo Woollen Mills 4 ply cotton
Colours: Sky, Blue Ice, Arctic and Parchment
Hook: 3.5 mm
Layout: 8 x 8 squares
Squares used: all patterns x 1

Embellished Zipper Pouch; Page 9
Yarn: Shibui Knits Reed linen
Colour: Ash
Hook: 4.5 mm
Square used: Banda Page 68

Embellished Apron; Page 88
Yarn: Shibui Knits Reed linen held double, Quince & Co Kestrel linen
Colours: Ash and Ebb Tide
Hook: 5mm
Square used: Sicily Page 42

Wrap; 43 x 170 cm; Page 12
Yarn: Great Ocean Road Woollen Mill La Bella alpaca and merino 4 ply
Colour: Grey
Hook: 6mm
Layout: 3 x 11 squares
Square used: Cortes Page 23

Four Colour Sampler Blanket; 125 x 125 cm; Pages 83, 89
Yarn: Bendigo Woollen Mills 8 ply cotton
Colours: Sky, Blue Ice, Arctic and Parchment
Hook: 4.5 mm
Layout: 8 x 8 squares
Squares used: all patterns x 1

Patterns

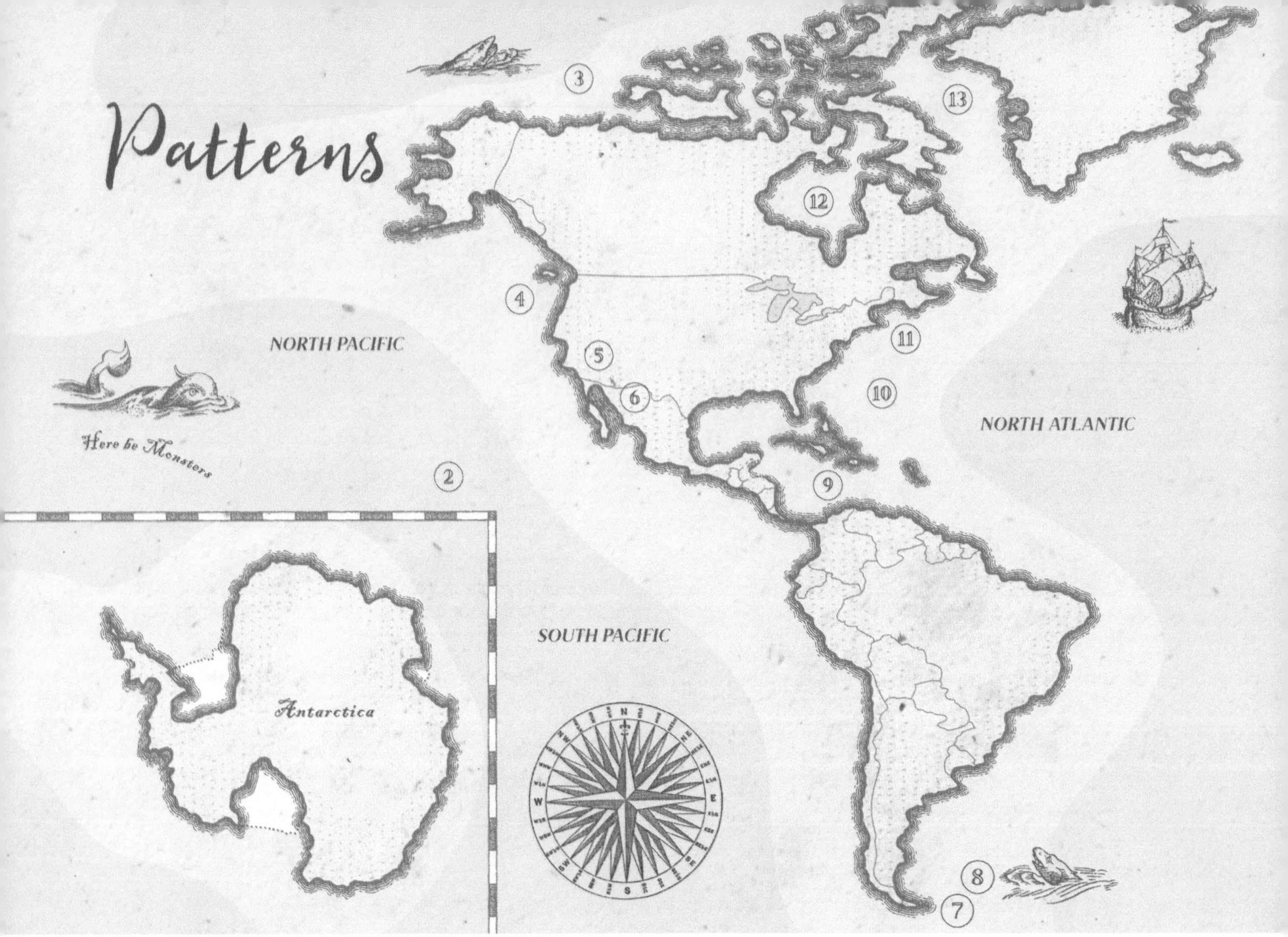

3
13
12
4
NORTH PACIFIC
11
5
6
10
NORTH ATLANTIC
Here be Monsters
2
9
SOUTH PACIFIC
Antarctica
8
7

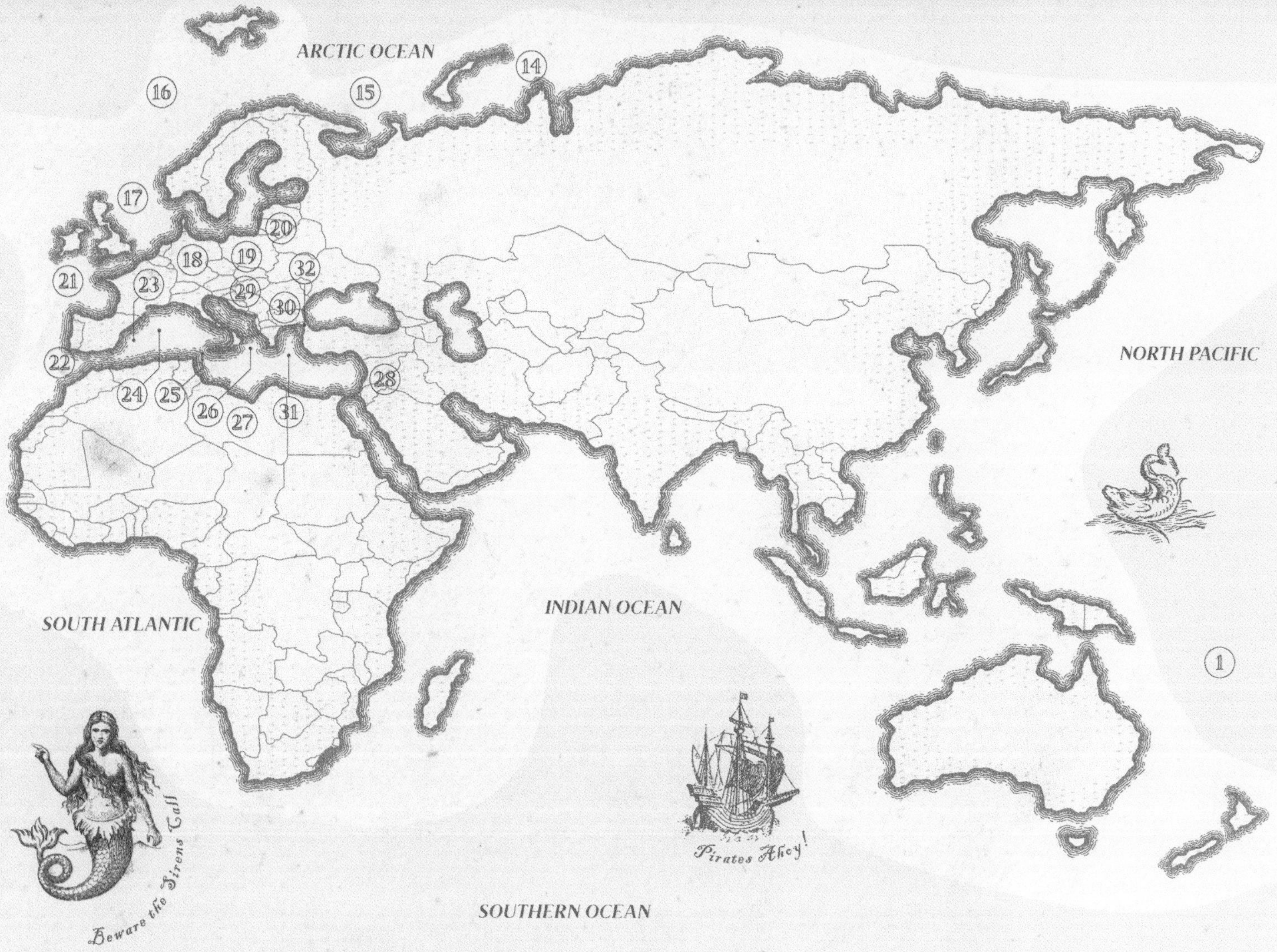

17.
Kattegat
Page 34

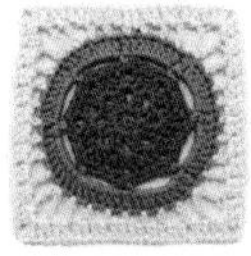
21.
Biscay
Page 38

25.
Sicily
Page 42

29.
Adriatic
Page 46

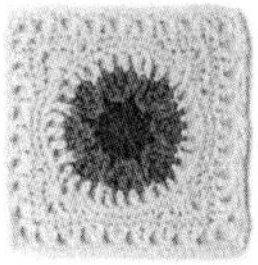
18.
Oresund
Page 35

22.
Alboran
Page 39

26.
Ionian
Page 43

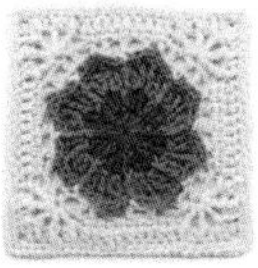
30.
Thracian
Page 47

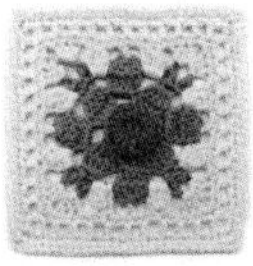
19.
Baltic
Page 36

23.
Catalan
Page 40

27.
Sidra
Page 44

31.
Aegean
Page 48

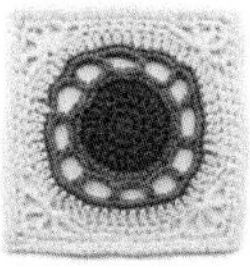
20.
Riga
Page 37

24.
Sardinia
Page 41

28.
Levantine
Page 45

32.
Marmara
Page 49

Patterns

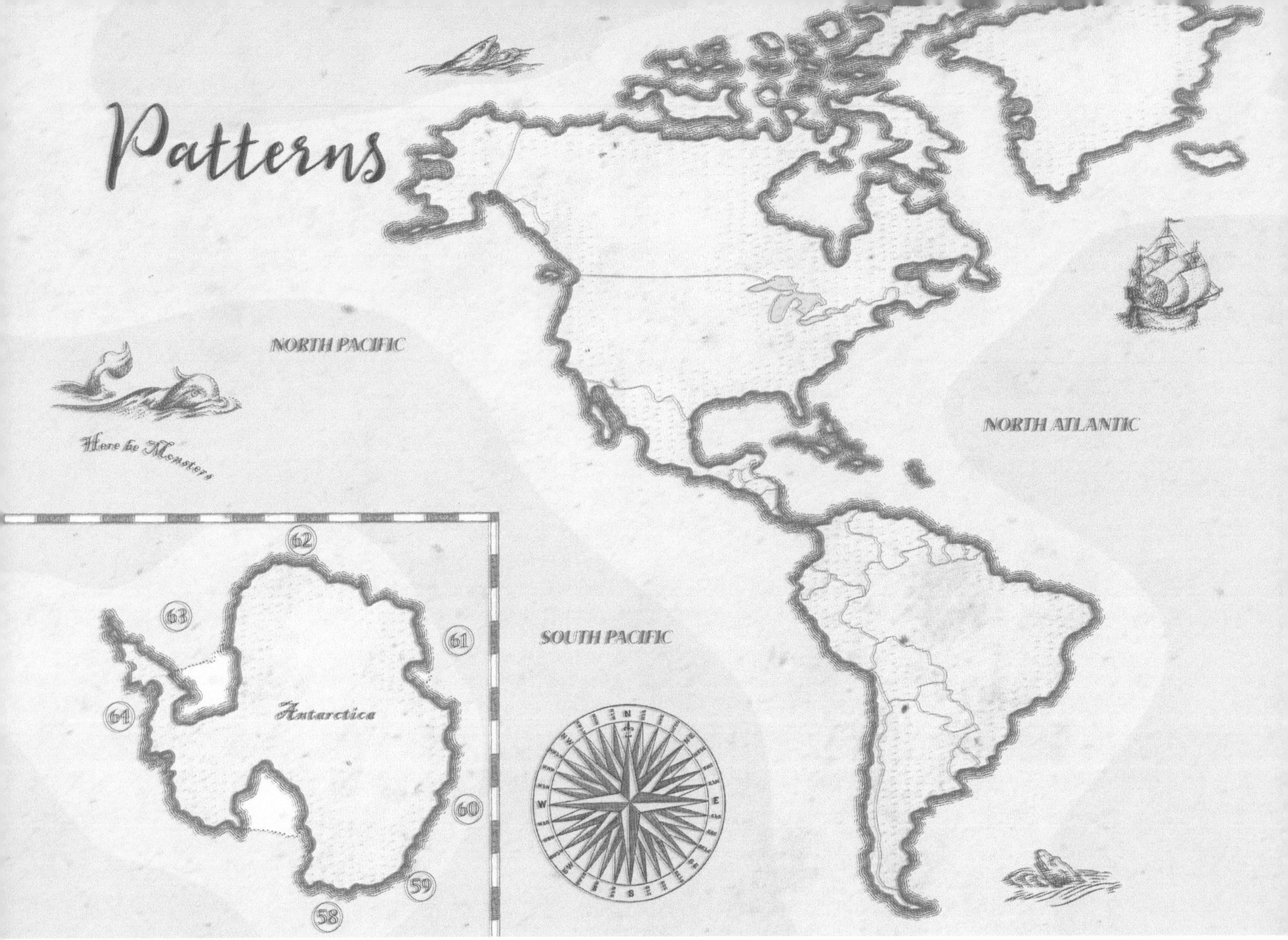
NORTH PACIFIC
Here be Monsters
NORTH ATLANTIC
SOUTH PACIFIC
Antarctica
62
63
61
64
60
59
58

ARCTIC OCEAN
NORTH PACIFIC
INDIAN OCEAN
SOUTH ATLANTIC
SOUTHERN OCEAN
33
34
35
36
37
38
39
40
41
42
43
44
45
46
47
48
49
50
51
52
53
54
55
56
57
Beware the Sirens Call
Pirates Ahoy!

KORO

Located in the Pacific Ocean, surrounded by the islands of the Fijian archipelago
Φ -17.681708, λ 179.706522

Using A, begin with mc.

R1: ch4 (stch), 2dtr, *ch2**, 3dtr*, rep from * to * 4x and * to ** 1x, join with ss to 4th ch of stch.
{18 sts, 6 2-ch sps}

R2: ch4 (stch), dtr2tog over next 2 sts, *ch3, 3dc in 2-ch sp, ch3**, dtr3tog over next 3 sts*, rep from * to * 4x and * to ** 1x, join with ss to top of dtr2tog. Fasten off.
{24 sts, 12 3-ch sps}

R3: Attach B with stdg dc to the top of any dtr3tog, *ch3, skip 3-ch sp, dtr in next 3 sts, ch3, skip 3-ch sp**, dc in next st*, rep from * to * 4x and * to ** 1x, join with ss to first st.
{24 sts, 12 3-ch sps}

R4: dc in same st as ss, *3dc in 3-ch sp, dc in next 3 sts, 3dc in 3-ch sp**, dc in next st*, rep from * to * 4x and * to ** 1x, join with ss to first st. Fasten off. {60 sts}

R5: Attach C with ss to any dc in a st above a dtr3tog, ch4 (stch), hdtr in same st, *tr in next 2 sts, htr in next 2 sts, dc in next 6 sts, htr in next 2 sts, tr in next 2 sts**, (hdtr, dtr, hdtr) in next st*, rep from * to * 2x and * to ** 1x, hdtr in same st as first sts, join with ss to 4th ch of stch. Fasten off.
{14 sts on each side; 4 3-st cnrs}

R6: Attach D with stdg tr to any dtr, ch1, tr in same st, *ch2, skip 2 sts, tr in next 2 sts, ch2, skip 2 sts, tr in next 4 sts, ch2, skip 2 sts, tr in next 2 sts, ch2, skip 2 sts**, (2x [tr, ch1], tr) in next st*, rep from * to * 2x and * to ** 1x, tr in same st as first sts, ch1, join with ss to first st.
{10 sts, 2 1-ch sps, 4 2-ch sps on each side; 4 1-st cnrs}

R7: dc in same st as ss, *dc in 1-ch sp, dc in next st, 2dc in 2-ch sp, dc in next 2 sts, 2dc in 2-ch sp, dc in next 4 sts, 2dc in 2-ch sp, dc in next 2 sts, 2dc in 2-ch sp, dc in next st, dc in 1-ch sp**, (dc, ch2, dc) in next st*, rep from * to * 2x and * to ** 1x, dc in same st as first st, ch2, join with ss to first st. Fasten off.
{22 sts on each side; 4 2-ch cnr sps}

PACIFIC

Between the Arctic Ocean in the north to the Antarctic in the south.
Φ -8.783195, λ -124.508522

Using A, begin with mc.

R1: ch3 (stch), 23tr, join with ss to 3rd ch of stch.
{24 sts}

R2: ch4 (stch), 4dtr in same st as ss, *skip 2 sts, htr in next st, skip 2 sts**, 9dtr in next st*, rep from * to * 2x and * to ** 1x, 4dtr in same st as first sts, join with ss to 4th ch of stch. Fasten off.
{1 st on each side; 4 9-st cnrs}

R3: Attach B with stdg dc to middle st of any 9-st cnr, *dc in lbv of next 4 sts, bptr around next st, dc in lbv of next 4 sts**, (dc, ch2, dc) in next st*, rep from * to * 2x and * to ** 1x, dc in same st as first st, ch1, join with dc to first st.
{11 sts on each side; 4 2-ch cnr sps}

R4: ch3 (stch), htr over joining dc, *htr in next 4 sts, skip 1 st, 5dtr in next st, skip 1 st, htr in next 4 sts**, (htr, tr, htr) in 2-ch sp*, rep from * to * 2x and * to ** 1x, htr in same sp as first sts, join with ss to 3rd ch of stch. Fasten off.
{13 sts on each side; 4 3-st cnrs}

R5: Attach C with stdg tr to middle st of any 3-st cnr, *tr in lbv of next 5 sts, htr in lbv of next st, dc in lbv of next 3 sts, htr in lbv of next st, tr in lbv of next 5 sts**, (tr, ch2, tr) in next st*, rep from * to * 2x and * to ** 1x, tr in same st as first st, ch1, join with dc to first st.
{17 sts on each side; 4 2-ch cnr sps}

R6: ch3 (stch), htr over joining dc, *htr in next 17 sts**, (htr, tr, htr) in 2-ch sp*, rep from * to * 2x and * to ** 1x, htr in same sp as first sts, join with ss to 3rd ch of stch. Fasten off.
{17 sts on each side; 4 3-st cnrs}

R7: Attach D with stdg dc to middle st of any 3-st cnr, *dc in lbv of next 19 sts**, (dc, ch2, dc) in next st*, rep from * to * 2x and * to ** 1x, dc in same st as first st, ch1, join with dc to first st.
{21 sts on each side; 4 2-ch cnr sps}

R8: dc over joining dc, *dc in next 21 sts**, (dc, ch2, dc) in 2-ch sp*, rep from * to * 2x and * to ** 1x, dc in same sp as first st, ch2, join with ss to first st. Fasten off.
{23 sts on each side; 4 2-ch cnr sps}

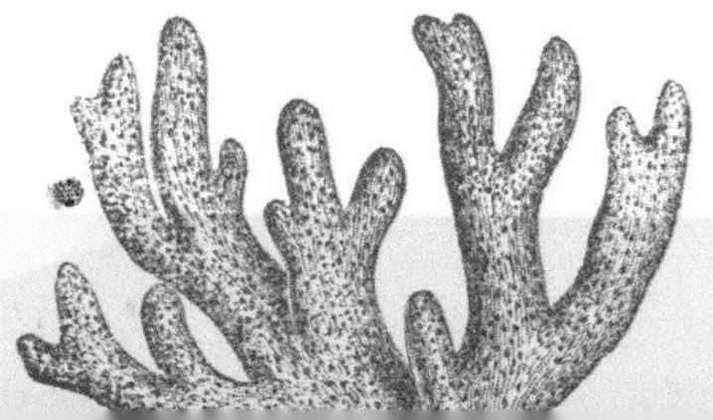

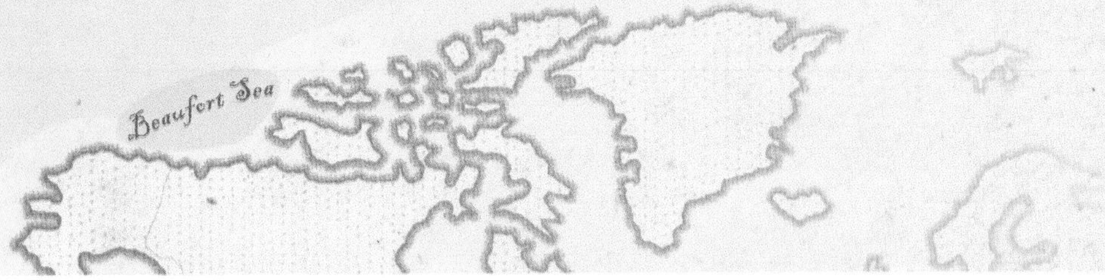

BEAUFORT

Located in the Arctic Ocean above
Alaska and Canada
Φ 71.658133, λ -135.650107

Using A, attach yarn to hook with a slip knot, ch1, work all R1 sts into that ch.

R1: ch3 (stch), 11tr, join with ss to 3rd ch of stch. {12 sts}

R2: ch3 (stch), fptr around same st ss'd into, *tr in next st, fptr around same st*, rep from * to * 10x, join with ss to 3rd ch of stch. Fasten off. {24 sts}

R3: Attach B with stdg dc to any tr (not fptr), dc in next st, *spike dc between sts of R1 below**, dc in next 2 sts*, rep from * to * 10x and * to ** 1x, join with ss to first st. {36 sts}

R4: ch3 (stch), tr in next st, *ch1, 3trcl in next st, ch1**, tr in next 2 sts*, rep from * to * 10x and * to ** 1x, join with ss to 3rd ch of stch. {36 sts, 24 1-ch sps}

R5: dc in same st as ss, dc in next st, *dc in 1-ch sp, fpdc around cluster, dc in 1-ch sp**, dc in next 2 sts*, rep from * to * 10x and * to ** 1x, join with ss to first st. Fasten off. {60 sts}

R6: Attach C with stdg tr to any st, tr in next 59 sts, join with ss to first st. {60 sts}

R7: ch3 (stch), 4trcl in same st as ss, *ch1, 5trcl in next st, ch1, skip 1 st, htr in next 2 sts, dc in next 6 sts, htr in next 2 sts, ch1, skip 1 st, 5trcl in next st, ch1**, 5trcl in next st*, rep from * to * 2x and * to ** 1x, join with ss to top of 4trcl. Fasten off.
{12 sts, 4 1-ch sps on each side; 4 1-cluster cnrs}

R8: Attach D with stdg dc to any cnr st, dc in same st, *dc in 1-ch sp, fpdc around cluster, spike dc in skipped st of R6 below, dc in next 10 sts, spike dc in skipped st of R6 below, fpdc around cluster, dc in 1-ch sp**, (2dc, ch2, 2dc) in next st*, rep from * to * 2x and * to ** 1x, 2dc in same st as first sts, ch1, join with dc to first st. {20 sts on each side; 4 2-ch cnr sps}

R9: dc over joining dc, *dc in next 20 sts**, (dc, ch2, dc) in 2-ch sp*, rep from * to * 2x and * to ** 1x, dc in same sp as first st, ch1, join with dc to first st. {22 sts on each side; 4 2-ch cnr sps}

R10: dc over joining dc, *dc in next 22 sts**, (dc, ch2, dc) in 2-ch sp*, rep from * to * 2x and * to ** 1x, dc in same sp as first st, ch2, join with ss to first st. Fasten off.
{24 sts on each side; 4 2-ch cnr sps}

SALISH

Located between Vancouver Island and Canada
Φ 48.299274, λ -123.044600

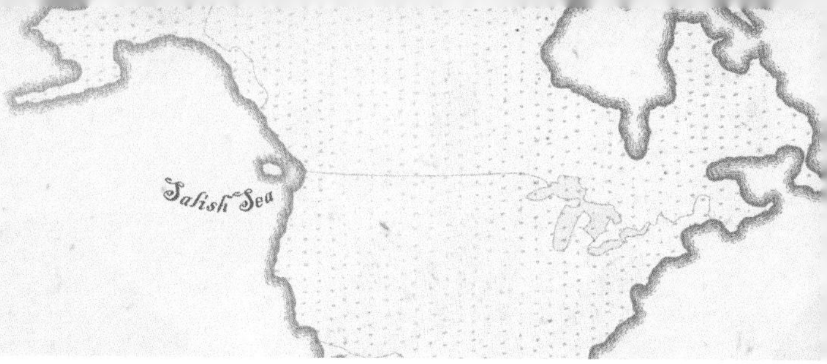

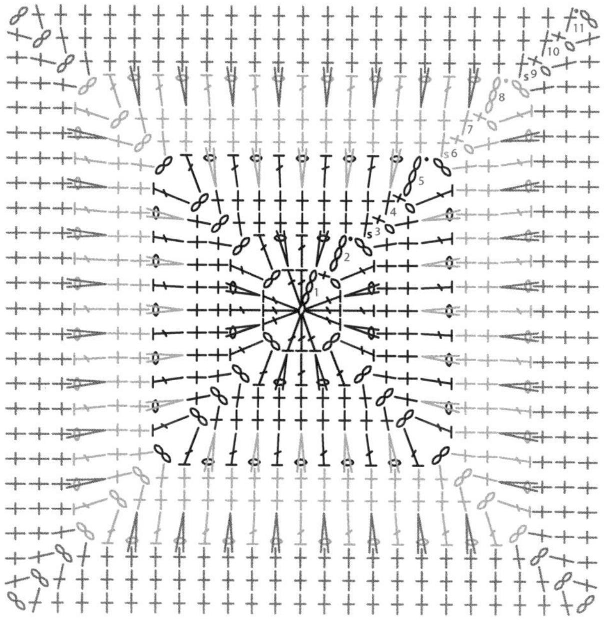

Using A, attach yarn to hook with a slip knot, ch1, work all R1 sts into that ch.

R1: ch3 (stch), 2tr, *ch2, 3tr*, rep from * to * 2x, ch1, join with dc to 3rd ch of stch.
{3 sts on each side; 4 2-ch cnr sps}

R2: ch3 (stch), *ch1, skip 1 st, tr in next st, ch1, skip 1 st**, (tr, ch2, tr) in 2-ch sp*, rep from * to * 2x and * to ** 1x, tr in same sp as first st, ch2, join with ss to 3rd ch of stch. Fasten off.
{3 sts, 2 1-ch sps on each side; 4 2-ch cnr sps}

R3: Attach B with a stdg dc to any 2-ch cnr sp, *2x [dc in next st, spike dc in skipped st of R1 below], dc in next st**, (dc, ch2, dc) in 2-ch sp*, rep from * to * 2x and * to ** 1x, dc in same sp as first st, ch1, join with dc to first st.
{7 sts on each side; 4 2-ch cnr sps}

R4: dc over joining dc, *dc in next 7 sts**, (dc, ch2, dc) in 2-ch sp*, rep from * to * 2x and * to ** 1x, dc in same sp as first st, ch1, join with dc to first st. {9 sts on each side; 4 2-ch cnr sps}

R5: ch3 (stch), *4x [ch1, skip 1 st, tr in next st], ch1, skip 1 st**, (tr, ch2, tr) in 2-ch sp*, rep from * to * 2x and * to ** 1x, tr in same sp as first st, ch2, join with ss to 3rd ch of stch. Fasten off.
{6 sts, 5 1-ch sps on each side; 4 2-ch cnr sps}

R6: Attach C with a stdg dc to any 2-ch cnr sp, *5x [dc in next st, spike dc in skipped st of R4 below], dc in next st**, (dc, ch2, dc) in 2-ch sp*, rep from * to * 2x and * to ** 1x, dc in same sp as first st, ch1, join with dc to first st.
{13 sts on each side; 4 2-ch cnr sps}

R7: dc over joining dc, *dc in next 13 sts**, (dc, ch2, dc) in 2-ch sp*, rep from * to * 2x and * to ** 1x, dc in same sp as first st, ch1, join with dc to first st. {15 sts on each side; 4 2-ch cnr sps}

R8: ch3 (stch), *7x [ch1, skip 1 st, tr in next st], ch1, skip 1 st**, (tr, ch2, tr) in 2-ch sp*, rep from * to * 2x and * to ** 1x, tr in same sp as first st, ch2, join with ss to 3rd ch of stch. Fasten off.
{9 sts, 8 1-ch sps on each side; 4 2-ch cnr sps}

R9: Attach D with a stdg dc to any 2-ch cnr sp, *8x [dc in next st, spike dc in skipped st of R7 below], dc in next st**, (dc, ch2, dc) in 2-ch sp*, rep from * to * 2x and * to ** 1x, dc in same sp as first st, ch1, join with dc to first st.
{19 sts on each side; 4 2-ch cnr sps}

R10: dc over joining dc, *dc in next 19 sts**, (dc, ch2, dc) in 2-ch sp*, rep from * to * 2x and * to ** 1x, dc in same sp as first st, ch1, join with dc to first st. {21 sts on each side; 4 2-ch cnr sps}

R11: dc over joining dc, *dc in next 21 sts**, (dc, ch2, dc) in next st*, rep from * to * 2x and * to ** 1x, dc in same sp as first st, ch2, join with ss to first st. Fasten off.
{23 sts on each side; 4 2-ch cnr sps}

SALTON

A saline lake located on the San Andreas Fault,
in the U.S. state of California
Φ 33.328617, λ -115.843414

Using A, begin with mc.

R1: ch3 (stch), *ch1, 5tr, ch1**, tr, ch2, tr*, rep from * to * 2x and * to ** 1x, tr, ch1, join with dc to 3rd ch of stch.
{7 sts, 2 1-ch sps on each side; 4 2-ch cnr sps}

R2: dc over joining dc, *dc in next st, dc in both 1-ch sps on either side of the next 5 sts at the same time, dc in next st**, (dc, ch2, dc) in 2-ch sp*, rep from * to * 2x and * to ** 1x, dc in same sp as first st, ch2, join with ss to first st. Fasten off.
{5 sts on each side; 4 2-ch cnr sps}

R3: Attach B with stdg tr to any 2-ch cnr sp, tr in same sp, *tr in next st, ch1, 5tr in next st, ch1, 2tr in next st, ch1, 5tr in next st, ch1, tr in next st**, (2tr, ch2, 2tr) in 2-ch sp*, rep from * to * 2x and * to ** 1x, 2tr in same sp as first sts, ch1, join with dc to first st.
{18 sts, 4 1-ch sps on each side; 4 2-ch cnr sps}

R4: dc over joining dc, *dc in next 3 sts, dc in both 1-ch sps on either side of the next 5 sts at the same time, dc in next 2 sts, dc in both 1-ch sps on either side of the 5tr together, dc in next 3 sts**, (dc, ch2, dc) in 2-ch sp*, rep from * to * 2x and * to ** 1x, dc in same sp as first st, ch2, join with ss to first st. Fasten off.
{12 sts on each side; 4 2-ch cnr sps}

R5: Attach C with stdg tr to any 2-ch cnr sp, *2x [ch1, skip 1 st, tr in next st], ch1, skip 1 st, tr in next 2 sts, 2x [ch1, skip 1 st, tr in next st], ch1, skip 1 st**, (tr, ch3, tr) in 2-ch sp*, rep from * to * 2x and * to ** 1x, tr in same sp as first st, ch1, join with htr to first st.
{8 sts, 6 1-ch sps on each side; 4 3-ch cnr sps}

R6: 2dc over joining htr, *3x [dc in next st, dc in 1-ch sp], dc2tog over next 2 sts, 3x [dc in 1-ch sp, dc in next st]**, (2dc, ch2, 2dc) in 3-ch sp*, rep from * to * 2x and * to ** 1x, 2dc in same sp as first sts, ch2, join with ss to first st. Fasten off.
{17 sts on each side; 4 2-ch cnr sps}

R7: Attach D with stdg tr to any 2-ch cnr sp, *tr in next 2 sts, ch2, tr5tog over next 5 sts, ch2, tr in next 3 sts, ch2, tr5tog over next 5 sts, ch2, tr in next 2 sts**, (tr, ch2, tr) in 2-ch sp*, rep from * to * 2x and * to ** 1x, tr in same sp as first st, ch1, join with dc to first st.
{11 sts, 4 2-ch sps on each side; 4 2-ch cnr sps}

R8: dc over joining dc, *dc in next 3 sts, 2dc in 2-ch sp, dc in next st, 2dc in 2-ch sp, dc in next 3 sts, 2dc in 2-ch sp, dc in next st, 2dc in 2-ch sp, dc in next 3 sts**, (dc, ch2, dc) in 2-ch sp*, rep from * to * 2x and * to ** 1x, dc in same sp as first st, ch1, join with dc to first st.
{21 sts on each side; 4 2-ch cnr sps}

R9: dc over joining dc, *dc in next 21 sts**, (dc, ch2, dc) in 2-ch sp*, rep from * to * 2x and * to ** 1x, dc in same sp as first st, ch2, join with ss to first st. Fasten off.
{23 sts on each side; 4 2-ch cnr sps}

CORTES

Separates the Baja Peninsula from Mexico
Φ 27.371766, λ -111.300689

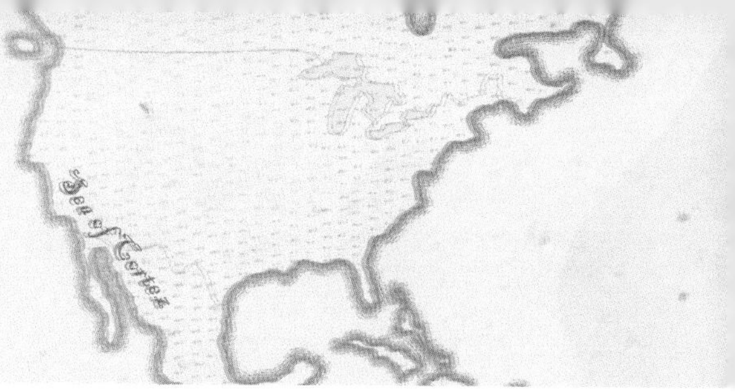

★ *pcl = point cluster: first and last legs of tr3tog are fp, middle leg is worked into st.*

Using A, begin with mc.

R1: ch3 (stch), 15tr, join with ss to 3rd ch of stch. Fasten off. {16 sts}

R2: Attach B with stdg tr to any st, 2tr in same st, *skip 1 st**, 3tr in next st*, rep from * to * 6x and * to ** 1x, join with ss to first st. {24 sts}

R3: ch3 (stch), tr2tog over next 2 sts, *ch2, tr between 3-st groups, ch2**, tr3tog over next 3 sts*, rep from * to * 6x and * to ** 1x, join with ss to top of tr2tog. Fasten off.
{16 sts, 16 2-ch sps}

R4: Attach C with stdg tr to any tr, *ch1, 3tr in 2-ch sp, ch1**, tr in next st*, rep from * to * 14x and * to ** 1x, join with ss to first st.
{64 sts, 32 1-ch sps}

R5: ch3 (stch), *ch2, skip 1-ch sp, pcl over next 3 sts, ch2, skip 1-ch sp**, tr in next st*, rep from * to * 14x and * to ** 1x, join with ss to 3rd ch of stch. {32 sts, 32 2-ch sps}

R6: dc in same st as ss, *2dc in 2-ch sp, skip 1 st, 2dc in 2-ch sp**, dc in next st*, rep from * to * 14x and * to ** 1x, join with ss to first st. Fasten off. {80 sts}

R7: Attach D with stdg dtr to any st above a tr of R5, 2x [ch1, dtr] in same st, *skip 3 sts, htr in next st, dc in next 11 sts, htr in next st, skip 3 sts**, (4x [dtr, ch1], dtr) in next st*, rep from * to * 2x and * to ** 1x, 2x [dtr, ch1] in same st as first sts, join with ss to first st.
{17 sts, 4 1-ch sps on each side; 4 1-st cnrs}

R8: dc in same st as ss, *dc in 1-ch sp, dc in next st, dc in 1-ch sp, dc in next 15 sts, dc in 1-ch sp, dc in next st, dc in 1-ch sp**, (dc, ch2, dc) in next st*, rep from * to * 2x and * to ** 1x, dc in same st as first st, ch2, join with ss to first st. Fasten off.
{23 sts on each side; 4 2-ch cnr sps}

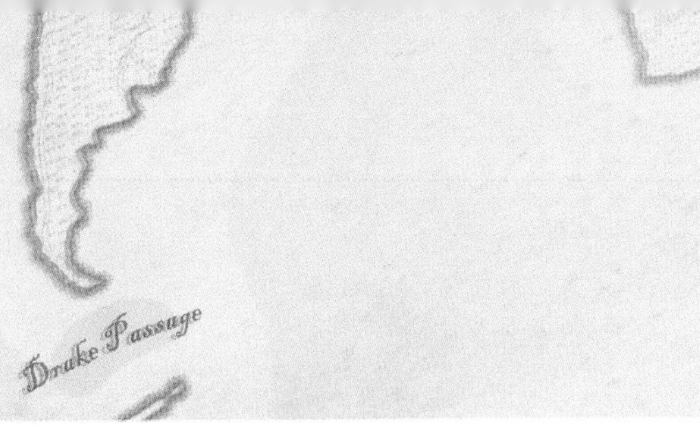

DRAKE

Located between South America's Cape Horn and the South Shetland Islands of Antarctica
Φ -59.445076, λ -63.163696

☆ *pcl = point cluster: first and last legs of tr3tog are fp, middle leg is worked into st.*

Using A, attach yarn to hook with a slip knot, ch1, work all R1 sts into that ch.

R1: ch3 (stch), *ch1**, tr*, rep from * to * 6x and * to ** 1x, join with ss to 3rd ch of stch. {8 sts, 8 1-ch sps}

R2: fpss around st ss'd into, ch3 (stch), tr in same st as ss, fptr around st just worked into, *skip 1-ch sp**, fptr around next st, tr in same st, fptr around same st*, rep from * to * 6x and * to ** 1x, join with ss to 3rd ch of stch. {24 sts}

R3: spike dc over ss join and into 1-ch sp of R1 below, *fptr around next st, 2tr in next st, fptr around next st**, spike dc between last and next st and into 1-ch sp of R1 below*, rep from * to * 6x and * to ** 1x, join with ss to first st. {40 sts}

R4: dc in same st as ss, *ch3, skip 4 sts**, dc in next st*, rep from * to * 6x and * to ** 1x, join with ss to first st. Fasten off. {8 sts, 8 3-ch sps}

R5: Attach B with stdg tr to any st, *ch1, 3tr in 3-ch sp, ch1**, tr in next st*, rep from * to * 6x and * to ** 1x, join with ss to first st. {32 sts, 16 1-ch sps}

R6: fpss around st ss'd into, ch3 (stch), tr in same st as ss, fptr around same st, *ch1, skip 1-ch sp, pcl over next 3 sts, ch1, skip 1-ch sp**, fptr around next st, tr in same st, fptr around same st*, rep from * to * 6x and * to ** 1x, join with ss to 3rd ch of stch. Fasten off. {32 sts, 16 1-ch sps}

R7: Attach C with stdg fpdc around any pcl, *skip 1-ch sp, fptr around next st, 3tr in next st, fptr around next st, skip 1-ch sp**, fpdc around next st*, rep from * to * 6x and * to ** 1x, join with ss to first st. {48 sts}

R8: ch3 (stch), 2tr in same st as ss, *fptr around next st, tr in next st, 3tr in next st, tr in next st, fptr around next st**, 3tr in next st*, rep from * to * 6x and * to ** 1x, join with ss to 3rd ch of stch. {80 sts}

R9: dc in same st as ss, dc in next 2 sts, *ch2, skip 3 sts, bpdc around next st, ch2, skip 3 sts**, dc in next 3 sts*, rep from * to * 6x and * to ** 1x, join with ss to first st. Fasten off. {32 sts, 16 2-ch sps}

R10: Attach D with stdg tr to middle dc of a 3-dc group, 2tr in same st, *tr in next st, 2htr in 2-ch sp, dc in next st, 2dc in 2-ch sp, dc in next 3 sts, 2dc in 2-ch sp, dc in next st, 2htr in 2-ch sp, tr in next st**, 5tr in next st*, rep from * to * 2x and * to ** 1x, 2tr in same st as first sts, join with ss to first st. {15 sts on each side; 4 5-st cnrs}

R11: dc in same st as ss, *dc in next 19 sts**, (dc, ch2, dc) in next st*, rep from * to * 2x and * to ** 1x, dc in same st as first st, ch1, join with dc to first st. {21 sts on each side; 4 2-ch cnr sps}

R12: dc over joining dc, *dc in next 21 sts**, (dc, ch2, dc) in 2-ch sp*, rep from * to * 2x and * to ** 1x, dc in same sp as first st, ch2, join with ss to first st. Fasten off. {23 sts on each side; 4 2-ch cnr sps}

SCOTIA

Located at the northern edge of the Southern Ocean at its boundary with the South Atlantic Ocean
Φ -61.572946, λ -56.411275

Using A, begin with mc.

R1: ch3 (stch), 4tr, *ch3, 5tr*, rep from * to * 2x, ch3, join with ss to 3rd ch of stch. Fasten off.
{20 sts and 4 3-ch cnr sps}

R2: Attach B with stdg tr to any 3-ch sp, ch2, tr in same sp, *skip 2 sts, (3tr, ch2, 3tr) in next st, skip 2 sts**, (2x [tr, ch2], tr) in 3-ch sp*, rep from * to * 2x and * to ** 1x, tr in same sp as first sts, ch2, join with ss to first st.
{8 sts, 3 2-ch sps on each side; 4 1-st cnrs}

R3: ch3 (stch), *ch2, tr in 2-ch sp, ch2, skip 1 st, tr3tog over next 3 sts, ch4, skip 2-ch sp, tr3tog over next 3 sts, ch2, skip 1 st, tr in 2-ch sp, ch2**, (tr, ch2, tr) in next st*, rep from * to * 2x and * to ** 1x, tr in same st as first st, ch2, join with ss to 3rd ch of stch. Fasten off.
{6 sts, 4 2-ch sps, 1 4-ch sp on each side; 4 2-ch cnr sps}

R4: Attach C with stdg tr to any 2-ch cnr sp, *2x [ch2, skip 1 st, tr in 2-ch sp], ch2, skip 1 st, 5tr in 2-ch sp of R2 below in front of 4-ch sp of R3, 2x [ch2, skip 1 st, tr in 2-ch sp], ch2, skip 1 st**, (tr, ch2, tr) in 2-ch sp*, rep from * to * 2x and * to ** 1x, tr in same sp as first st, ch1, join with dc to first st.
{11 sts, 6 2-ch sps on each side; 4 2-ch cnr sps}

R5: ch3 (stch), *2x [ch2, skip 1 st, tr in 2-ch sp], ch2, skip 1 st, tr in both 2-ch sps on either side of the next 5 sts at the same time, 2x [ch2, skip 1 st, tr in 2-ch sp], ch2, skip 1 st**, (tr, ch2, tr) in 2-ch sp*, rep from * to * 2x and * to ** 1x, tr in same sp as first st, ch2, join with ss to 3rd ch of stch. Fasten off.
{7 sts, 6 2-ch sps on each side; 4 2-ch cnr sps}

R6: Attach D with ss to any 2-ch cnr sp, ch3 (stch), *6x [tr in next st, 2tr in 2-ch sp]. tr in next st**, (tr, ch2, tr) in 2-ch sp*, rep from * to * 2x and * to ** 1x, tr in same sp as first st, ch2, join with ss to 3rd ch of stch. Fasten off.
{21 sts on each side; 4 2-ch cnr sps}

CARIBBEAN

Located to the south of Cuba, and the north of South America
Φ 14.540111, λ -74.967636

Using A, attach yarn to hook with a slip knot, ch1, work all R1 sts into that ch.

R1: ch3 (stch), *ch2, 5trcl, ch2**, tr*, rep from * to * 2x and * to ** 1x, join with ss to 3rd ch of stch. {8 sts, 8 2-ch sps}

R2: ch3 (stch), *ch2, 5trcl in 2-ch sp, ch2, fptr around next st, ch2, 5trcl in 2-ch sp, ch2**, tr in next st*, rep from * to * 2x and * to ** 1x, join with ss to 3rd ch of stch. Fasten off. {16 sts, 16 2-ch sps}

R3: Attach B with stdg tr to any tr (not fptr or 5trcl) *ch3, skip 2-ch sp, fptr around next st, ch3, skip (2-ch sp, 1 st and 2-ch sp), fptr around next st, ch3, skip 2-ch sp**, (tr, ch2, tr) in next st*, rep from * to * 2x and * to ** 1x, tr in same st as first st, ch1, join with dc to first st.
{4 sts, 3 3-ch sps on each side; 4 2-ch cnr sps}

R4: dc over joining dc, *3x [dc in next st, 3dc in 3-ch sp], dc in next st**, (dc, ch2, dc) in 2-ch sp*, rep from * to * 2x and * to ** 1x, dc in same sp as first st, ch2, join with ss to first st. Fasten off.
{15 sts on each side; 4 2-ch cnr sps}

R5: Attach C with stdg tr to any 2-ch cnr sp, *5x [ch2, tr2tog over the next 3 sts skipping the middle st], ch2**, (tr, ch2, tr) in 2-ch sp*, rep from * to * 2x and * to ** 1x, tr in same sp as first st, ch1, join with dc to first st.
{7 sts, 6 2-ch sps on each side; 4 2-ch cnr sps}

R6: dc over joining dc, *dc in next st, 5x [2dc in 2-ch sp, fpdc around next st], 2dc in 2-ch sp, dc in next st**, (dc, ch2, dc) in 2-ch sp*, rep from * to * 2x and * to ** 1x, dc in same sp as first st, ch1, join with dc to first st.
{21 sts on each side; 4 2-ch cnr sps}

R7: ch3 (stch), *ch1, skip 1 st, tr in next st, 5x [skip 2 sts, (tr, ch1, tr) in next st], skip 2 sts, tr in next st, ch1, skip 1 st**, (tr, ch2, tr) in 2-ch sp*, rep from * to * 2x and * to ** 1x, tr in same sp as first st, ch2, join with ss to 3rd ch of stch. Fasten off.
{9 sts, 2 1-ch sps on each side; 4 2-ch cnr sps}

R8: Attach D with stdg dc to any 2-ch cnr sp, *dc in next st, dc in 1-ch sp, 5x [dc in next 2 sts, dc in 1-ch sp], dc in next 2 sts, dc in 1-ch sp, dc in next st**, (dc, ch2, dc) in 2-ch sp*, dc in same sp as first st, ch2, join with ss to first st. Fasten off.
{23 sts on each side; 4 2-ch cnr sps}

SARGASSO

Located in the North Atlantic
Φ 30.811685, λ -55.461351

Using A, begin with mc.

R1: ch3 (stch), 2tr, *ch2, dc, ch2**, 3tr*, rep from * to * 2x and * to ** 1x, join with ss to 3rd ch of stch. {16 sts, 8 2-ch sps}

R2: ch3 (stch), tr2tog over next 2 sts, *ch3, skip 2-ch sp, fptr around next st, ch3, skip 2-ch sp**, tr3tog over next 3 sts*, rep from * to * 2x and * to ** 1x, join with ss to top of tr2tog. Fasten off. {8 sts, 8 3-ch sps}

R3: Attach B with stdg dc to any tr3tog, *(dc, htr, tr, hdtr) in 3-ch sp, dtr in next st, (hdtr, tr, htr, dc) in 3-ch sp**, dc in next st*, rep from * to * 2x and * to ** 1x, join with ss to first st. Fasten off. {40 sts}

R4: Attach C with stdg dtr to middle dc of any 3-dc group, *ch2, skip 1 st, tr in next st, ch2, skip 2 sts, dc in next st, ch2, skip 2 sts, tr in next st, ch2, skip 1 st**, dtr in next st*, rep from * to * 2x and * to ** 1x, join with ss to first st. {16 sts, 16 2-ch sps}

R5: ch3 (stch), 3tr in same st as ss, *dc in 2-ch sp, 2x [dc in next st, 2dc in 2-ch sp], dc in next st, dc in 2-ch sp**, 7tr in next st*, rep from * to * 2x and * to ** 1x, 3tr in same st as first sts, join with ss to 3rd ch of stch. {9 sts on each side; 4 7-st cnrs}

R6: 2dc in same st as ss, *dc in next 3 sts, ch4, skip 4 sts, htr in next st, ch4, skip 4 sts, dc in next 3 sts**, 3dc in next st*, rep from * to * 2x and * to ** 1x, dc in same st as first sts, join with ss to first st. {7 sts, 2 4-ch sps on each side; 4 3-st cnrs}

R7: 2dc in same st as ss, *dc in next 4 sts, 4dc in 4-ch sp, dc in next st, 4dc in 4-ch sp, dc in next 4 sts**, 3dc in next st*, rep from * to * 2x and * to ** 1x, dc in same st as first sts, join with ss to first st. Fasten off. {17 sts on each side; 4 3-st cnrs}

R8: Attach D with stdg tr to middle st of any 3-st cnr, tr in same st, *tr in blo of next 19 sts**, (2tr, ch1, 2tr) in next st*, rep from * to * 2x and * to ** 1x, 2tr in same st as first sts, join with dc to first st. {23 sts on each side; 4 1-ch cnr sps}

R9: dc over joining dc, *dc in next 23 sts**, (dc, ch2, dc) in 1-ch sp*, rep from * to * 2x & * to ** 1x, dc in same sp as first st, ch2, join with ss to first st. Fasten off. {25 sts on each side; 4 2-ch cnr sps}

MAINE

A large gulf of the Atlantic Ocean on the east coast of North America
Φ 42.863081, λ -68.263659

Using A, begin with mc.

R1: ch3 (stch), 4tr, *ch1, 5tr*, rep from * to * 6x, join with dc to 3rd ch of stch. Pull mc tight.
{40 sts, 8 1-ch sps}

R2: dc over joining dc and in 1-ch sp after the next 5 sts at the same time, *ch3**, dc in both 1-ch sps on either side of the next 5 sts at the same time*, rep from * to * 6x and * to ** 1x, join with ss to first st. Fasten off. {8 sts, 8 3-ch sps}

R3: Attach B with stdg fptr around any st, tr in same st, fptr around same st, *ch1, 5tr in 3-ch sp, ch1**, fptr around next st, tr in same st, fptr around same st*, rep from * to * 6x, and * to ** 1x, join with ss to first st. {64 sts, 16 1-ch sps}

R4: ss to next st, ch3 (stch), 4tr in same st, *ch5, skip (1 st, 1-ch sp, 5tr, 1-ch sp, 1 st)**, 5tr in next st*, rep from * to * 6x and * to ** 1x, ch4, join with dc to 3rd ch of stch. {40 sts, 8 5-ch sps}

R5: dc over joining dc and in next 5-ch sp at the same time, *2dc in 5-ch sp, htr in 5-ch sp and into middle st of 5tr below from R3, 2dc in 5-ch sp**, dc in both the 5-ch sps on either side of the next 5 sts at the same time*, rep from * to * 6x and * to ** 1x, join with ss to first st. Fasten off.
{48 sts}

R6: Attach C with ss to any st that gathered 5 sts together, ch3 (stch), 2tr in same st, *skip 2 sts, htr in next 7 sts, skip 2 sts**, (3tr, ch1, 3tr) in next st*, rep from * to * 2x and * to ** 1x, 3tr in same st as first sts, ch1, join with ss to 3rd ch of stch. Fasten off.
{13 sts on each side; 4 1-ch cnr sps}

R7: Attach D with stdg tr to any 1-ch cnr sp, *tr in lbv of next 13 sts**, (tr, ch2, tr) in 1-ch sp*, rep from * to * 2x and * to ** 1x, tr in same sp as first st, ch1, join with dc to first st.
{15 sts on each side; 4 2-ch cnr sps}

R8: ch3 (stch), *fptr around next 15 sts**, (tr, ch2, tr) in 2-ch sp*, rep from * to * 2x and * to ** 1x, tr in same sp as first st, ch1, join with dc to 3rd ch of stch. {17 sts on each side; 4 2-ch cnr sps}

R9: ch3 (stch), *fptr around next 17 sts**, (tr, ch2, tr) in 2-ch sp*, rep from * to * 2x and * to ** 1x, tr in same sp as first st, ch2, join with ss to 3rd ch of stch. Fasten off.
{19 sts on each side; 4 2-ch cnr sps}

HUDSON

A large body of saltwater in northeastern Canada
Φ 52.246638, λ -80.063360

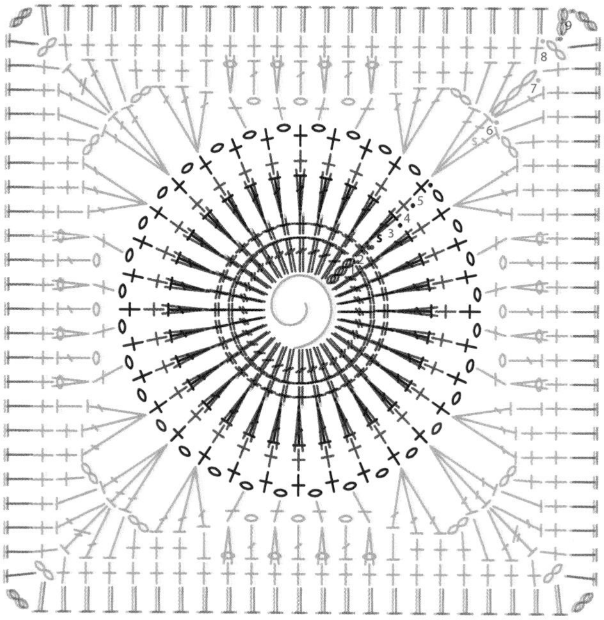

Using A, begin with mc.

R1: ch3 (stch), 31tr, join with ss to 3rd ch of stch. Close mc until hole is about an inch across. {32 sts}

R2: dc in same st as ss, dc in next 31 sts, join with ss to first st. Fasten off. {32 sts}

R3: Attach B with stdg tr to any st, tr in next 31 sts, join with ss to first st. {32 sts}

R4: spike dc into R2 st below, spike dc into next 31 sts of R2, join with ss to first st. {32 sts}

R5: dc in same st as ss, *ch1, dc in next st*, rep from * to * 30x, ch1, join with ss to first st. Fasten off. {32 sts, 32 1-ch sps}

R6: Attach C with stdg tr to any st, tr in same st, *ch2, skip 1-ch sp, 3tr in next st, skip (1-ch sp and 1 st), 3x [dc in 1-ch sp, ch1, skip 1 st], dc in 1-ch sp, skip (1 st and 1-ch sp), 3tr in next st, ch2, skip 1-ch sp**, 3tr in next st*, rep from * to * 2x and * to ** 1x, tr in same st as first sts, join with ss to first st.
{10 sts, 3 1-ch sps, 2 2-ch sps on each side; 4 3-st cnrs}

R7: ch3 (stch), tr in same st as ss, *htr in next st, dc in 2-ch sp, dc in next 2 sts, htr in next st, 3x [ch1, skip 1 st, tr in 1-ch sp], ch1, skip 1 st, htr in next st, dc in next 2 sts, dc in 2-ch sp, htr in next st**, (tr, hdtr, tr) in next st*, rep from * to * 2x and * to ** 1x, tr in same st as first sts, join with ss to 3rd ch of stch.
{13 sts, 4 1-ch sps on each side; 4 3-st cnrs}

R8: dc in same st as ss, *dc in next 6 sts, 3x [spike dc in skipped st of R6 below, dc in next st], spike dc in skipped st of R6 below, dc in next 6 sts**, (dc, ch2, dc) in next st*, rep from * to * 2x and * to ** 1x, dc in same st as first st, ch2, join with ss to first st. Fasten off.
{21 sts on each side; 4 2-ch cnr sps}

R9: Attach D with ss to any 2-ch cnr sp, ch2 (stch), *htr in next 21 sts**, (htr, ch2, htr) in 2-ch sp*, rep from * to * 2x and * to ** 1x, htr in same sp as first st, ch2, join with ss to 2nd ch of stch. Fasten off. {23 sts on each side; 4 2-ch cnr sps}

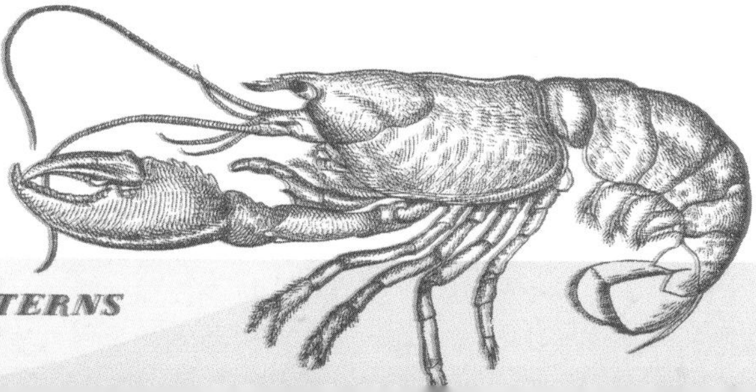

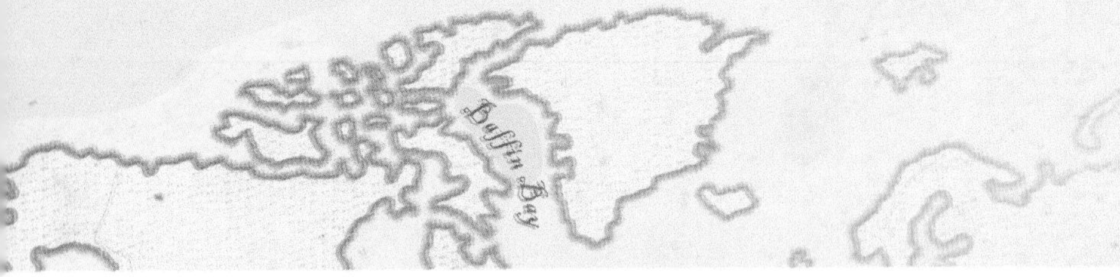

BAFFIN

Located between Baffin Island and the
west coast of Greenland
Φ 74.693253, λ -68.492805

Using A, ch8, join last ch to first with a ss over the top 2 strands of the first ch.

R1: ch3 (stch), tr in same st as ss, 2tr in next 7 chs over top 2 strands of each ch, join with ss to 3rd ch of stch. {16 sts}

R2: ch3 (stch), fptr around same st ss'd into, *tr in next st, fptr around same st*, rep from * to * 6x, join with ss to 3rd ch of stch. {32 sts}

R3: dc in same st as ss, dc in next 31 sts, join with ss to first st. Fasten off. {32 sts}

R4: Attach B with stdg tr to any st, *tr in next st, ch8, skip 5 sts, tr in next st**, (tr, ch2, tr) in next st*, rep from * to * 2x and * to ** 1x, tr in same st as first st, ch1, join with dc to first st.
{4 sts, 1 8-ch sp on each side; 4 2-ch cnr sps}

R5: ch3 (stch), tr over joining dc, *bptr around next 2 sts, dc in next 3 chs, 2 spike dc in middle skipped st of R4 below, dc in last 3 chs, bptr around next 2 sts**, 3tr in 2-ch sp*, rep from * to * 2x and * to ** 1x, tr in same sp as first sts, join with ss to 3rd ch of stch.
{12 sts on each side; 4 3-st cnrs}

R6: ch3 (stch), *tr in next 6 sts, tr2tog over next 2 sts, tr in next 6 sts**, (tr, ch2, tr) in next st*, rep from * to * 2x and * to ** 1x, tr in same st as first st, ch2, join with ss to 3rd ch of stch. Fasten off.
{15 sts on each side; 4 2-ch cnr sps}

R7: Attach C with stdg tr to any 2-ch cnr sp, *bptr around next 15 sts**, (tr, ch2, tr) in 2-ch sp*, rep from * to * 2x and * to ** 1x, tr in same sp as first st, ch1, join with dc to first st.
{17 sts on each side; 4 2-ch cnr sps}

R8: ch3 (stch), *8x [ch1, skip 1 st, tr in next st], ch1, skip 1 st**, (tr, ch2, tr) in 2-ch sp*, rep from * to * 2x and * to ** 1x, tr in same sp as first st, ch2, join with ss to 3rd ch of stch. Fasten off.
{10 sts, 9 1-ch sps on each side; 4 2-ch cnr sps}

R9: Attach D with stdg dc to any 2-ch cnr sp, *9x [dc in next st, spike dc in skipped st of R8 below], dc in next st**, (dc, ch2, dc) in 2-ch sp*, rep from * to * 2x and * to ** 1x, dc in same sp as first st, ch2, join with ss to first st. Fasten off.
{21 sts on each side; 4 2-ch cnr sps}

KARA

Located in the Arctic Ocean north of Siberia
Φ 75.311114, λ 74.761481

Using A, begin with mc.

R1: ch4 (stch), 2dtr, *ch3, dc, ch3**, 3dtr*, rep from * to * 2x and * to ** 1x, join with ss to 4th ch of stch. Pull mc closed tightly. Fasten off.
{16 sts, 8 3-ch sps}

R2: Attach B with a stdg dtr3tog over any 3-st group, *ch5, dc in 3-ch sp, ch3, skip 1 st, dc in 3-ch sp, ch5**, dtr3tog over next 3 sts*, rep from * to * 2x and * to ** 1x, join with ss to top of first st. {12 sts, 4 3-ch sps, 8 5-ch sps}

R3: dc in same st as ss, *ch5, skip (5-ch sp and 1 st), 4tr in 3-ch sp, ch5, skip (1 st and 5-ch sp)**, (dc, ch2, dc) in next st*, rep from * to * 2x and * to ** 1x, dc in same st as first st, ch2, join with ss to first st. Fasten off.
{6 sts, 2 5-ch sps on each side; 4 2-ch cnr sps}

R4: Attach C with stdg tr to any 2-ch cnr sp, 2tr in same sp, *skip 1 st, dc in 5-ch sp, ch4, tr4tog over next 4 sts, ch4, dc in 5-ch sp, skip 1 st**, 5tr in 2-ch sp*, rep from * to * 2x and * to ** 1x, 2tr in same sp as first sts, join with ss to first st.{3 sts, 2 4-ch sps on each side; 4 5-st cnrs}

R5: ch3 (stch), tr3tog over next 3 sts, *ch3, 2dc in 4-ch sp, dc in next st, 2dc in 4-ch sp, ch3**, tr4tog over next 4 sts, ch4, tr4tog beginning in the same st the last leg of the previous tr4tog was worked into*, rep from * to * 2x and * to ** 1x, tr4tog over the next 4 sts (the last leg will be in the st at the base of the stch), ch4, join with ss to top of tr3tog. Fasten off.
{7 sts, 2 3-ch sps on each side; 4 4-ch cnr sps}

R6: Attach D with stdg tr to any 4-ch cnr sp, 2tr in same sp, *tr in next st, 3tr in 3-ch sp, tr in next 5 sts, 3tr in 3-ch sp, tr in next st**, (3tr, ch2, 3tr) in 4-ch sp*, rep from * to * 2x and * to ** 1x, 3tr in same sp as first sts, ch1, join with dc to first st. {19 sts on each side; 4 2-ch cnr sps}

R7: dc over joining dc, *dc in next 19 sts**, (dc, ch2, dc) in 2-ch sp*, rep from * to * 2x and * to ** 1x, dc in same sp as first st, ch2, join with ss to first st. Fasten off.
{21 sts on each side; 4 2-ch cnr sps}

PECHORA

Located in the North Atlantic above the north west of Russia Φ 69.571361, λ 56.471102

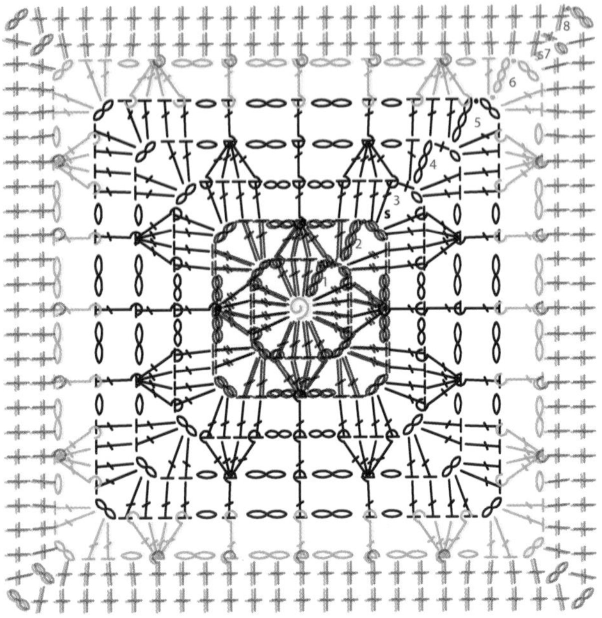

★ *pcl = point cluster: first and last legs of tr3tog are fp, middle leg is worked into st.*

Using A, begin with mc.

R1: ch3 (stch), 3tr, *ch2, 4tr*, rep from * to * 2x, ch1, join with dc to 3rd ch of stch. {16 sts, 4 2-ch cnr sps}

R2: ch3 (stch), tr over joining dc, *ch2, pcl over next 4 sts, ch2**, (2tr, ch2, 2tr) in 2-ch sp, rep from * to * 2x and * to ** 1x, 2tr in same sp as first sts, ch2, join with ss to 3rd ch of stch. Fasten off.
{5 sts, 2 2-ch sps on each side; 4 2-ch cnr sps}

R3: Attach B with stdg tr to any 2-ch cnr sp, tr in same sp, *tr in next 2 sts, ch2, skip 2-ch sp, fptr around next st, ch2, skip 2-ch sp, tr in next 2 sts**, (2tr, ch2, 2tr) in 2-ch sp*, rep from * to * 2x and * to ** 1x, 2tr in same sp as first sts, ch1, join with dc to first st.
{9 sts, 2 2-ch sps on each side; 4 2-ch cnr sps}

R4: ch3 (stch), tr over joining dc, *ch1, pcl over next 4 sts, ch2, skip 2-ch sp, fptr around next st, ch2, skip 2-ch sp, pcl over next 4 sts, ch1**, (2tr, ch2, 2tr) in 2-ch sp*, rep from * to * 2x and * to ** 1x, 2tr in same sp as first sts, ch1, join with dc to 3rd ch of stch.
{7 sts, 2 1-ch sps, 2 2-ch sps on each side; 4 2-ch cnr sps}

R5: ch3 (stch), tr over joining dc, *tr in next 2 sts, ch1, skip 1-ch sp, 2x [fptr around next st, ch2, skip 2-ch sp], fptr around next st, ch1, skip 1-ch sp, tr in next 2 sts**, (2tr, ch2, 2tr) in 2-ch sp*, rep from * to * 2x and * to ** 1x, 2tr in same sp as first sts, ch2, join with ss to 3rd ch of stch. Fasten off.
{11 sts, 2 1-ch sps, 2 2-ch sps on each side; 4 2-ch cnr sps}

R6: Attach C with ss to any 2-ch cnr sp, ch3 (stch), tr in same sp, *ch1, pcl over next 4 sts, ch2, skip 1-ch sp, 2x [fptr around next st, ch2, skip 2-ch sp], fptr around next st, ch2, skip 1-ch sp, pcl over next 4 sts, ch1**, (2tr, ch2, 2tr) in 2-ch sp*, rep from * to * 2x and * to ** 1x, 2tr in same sp as first sts, ch1, join with dc to 3rd ch of stch. Fasten off.
{9 sts, 2 1-ch sps, 4 2-ch sps on each side; 4 2-ch cnr sps}

R7: Attach D with stdg dc to any 2-ch cnr sp, *dc in next 2 sts, dc in 1-ch sp, 4x [fpdc around next st, 2dc in 2-ch sp], fpdc around next st, dc in 1-ch sp, dc in next 2 sts**, (dc, ch2, dc) in 2-ch sp*, rep from * to * 2x and * to ** 1x, dc in same sp as first st, ch1, join with dc to first st.
{21 sts on each side; 4 2-ch cnr sps}

R8: dc over joining dc, *dc in next 21 sts**, (dc, ch2, dc) in 2-ch sp*, rep from * to * 2x and * to ** 1x, dc in same sp as first st, ch2, join with ss to first st. Fasten off.
{23 sts on each side; 4 2-ch cnr sps}

NORWEGIAN

Located northwest of Norway between the North Sea and the Greenland Sea
Φ 70.798476, λ 4.497699

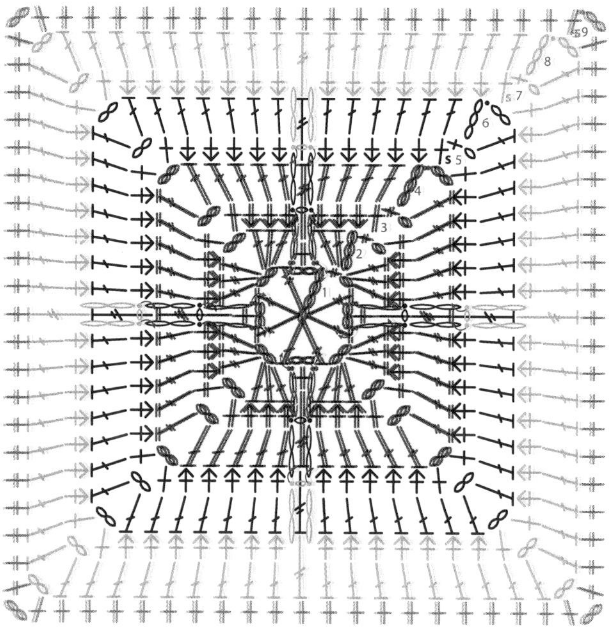

Using A, attach yarn to hook with a slip knot, ch1, work all R1 sts into that ch.

R1: ch3 (stch), *ch2, tr*, rep from * to * 6x, ch1, join with dc to 3rd ch of stch. {8 sts, 8 2-ch sps}

R2: ch3 (stch), 2tr over joining dc, *skip 1 st, dc in 2-ch sp, skip 1 st**, (3tr, ch2, 3tr) in 2-ch sp*, rep from * to * 2x and * to ** 1x, 3tr in same sp as first sts, ch1, join with dc to 3rd ch of stch. {7 sts on each side; 4 2-ch cnr sps}

R3: dc over joining dc, *dc in lbv of next 3 sts, ch2, ss around next st of R1 below, ss around next st of R1, ch2, skip 1 st of R2, dc in lbv of next 3 sts**, (dc, ch2, dc) in 2-ch sp*, rep from * to * 2x and * to ** 1x, dc in same sp as first st, ch1, join with dc to first st.
{8 sts, 2 2-ch sps, 2 ss on each side; 4 2-ch cnr sps}

R4: ch3 (stch), *tr in next 4 sts, hdtr in skipped st of R2 below, tr in next 4 sts**, (tr, ch2, tr) in 2-ch sp*, rep from * to * 2x and * to ** 1x, tr in same sp as first st, ch2, join with ss to 3rd ch of stch. Fasten off. {11 sts on each side; 4 2-ch cnr sps}

R5: Attach B with stdg dc to any 2-ch cnr sp, *dc in lbv of next 5 sts, ch2, ss around 2-ch sp of R3 below, ch1, ss around next 2-ch sp of R3, ch2, skip 1 st of R4, dc in lbv of next 5 sts**, (dc, ch2, dc) in 2-ch sp*, rep from * to * 2x and * to ** 1x, dc in same sp as first st, ch1, join with dc to first st.
{12 sts, 2 2-ch sps, 2 ss, 1 1-ch sp on each side; 4 2-ch cnr sps}

R6: ch3 (stch), *tr in next 6 sts, hdtr in skipped st of R4 below, tr in next 6 sts**, (tr, ch2, tr) in 2-ch sp*, rep from * to * 2x and * to ** 1x, tr in same sp as first st, ch2, join with ss to 3rd ch of stch. Fasten off. {15 sts on each side; 4 2-ch cnr sps}

R7: Attach C with stdg dc to any 2-ch cnr sp, *dc in lbv of next 7 sts, ch2, ss around 2-ch sp of R5 below, ch1, ss around next 2-ch sp of R5, ch2, skip 1 st of R6, dc in lbv of next 7 sts**, (dc, ch2, dc) in 2-ch sp*, rep from * to * 2x and * to ** 1x, dc in same sp as first st, ch1, join with dc to first st.
{16 sts, 2 2-ch sps, 2 ss, 1 1-ch sp on each side; 4 2-ch cnr sps}

R8: ch3 (stch), *tr in next 8 sts, hdtr in skipped st of R6 below, tr in next 8 sts**, (tr, ch2, tr) in 2-ch sp*, rep from * to * 2x and * to ** 1x, tr in same sp as first st, ch2, join with ss to 3rd ch of stch. Fasten off. {19 sts on each side; 4 2-ch cnr sps}

R9: Attach D with stdg dc to any 2-ch cnr sp, *dc in next 19 sts**, (dc, ch2, dc) in 2-ch sp*, rep from * to * 2x and * to ** 1x, dc in same sp as first st, ch2, join with ss to first st. Fasten off.
{21 sts on each side; 4 2-ch cnr sps}

KATTEGAT

Located between Denmark and Sweden
Φ 56.952164, λ 11.496607

Using A, attach yarn to hook with a slip knot, ch1, work all R1 sts into that ch.

R1: ch1, 12dc, join with ss to first st. {12 sts}

R2: dc in same st as ss, *dc in next 2 sts**, (dc, ch4, dc) in next st*, rep from * to * 2x and * to ** 1x, dc in same st as first st, ch1, join with tr to first st. {4 sts on each side; 4 4-ch cnr sps}

R3: 2dc over joining tr, *skip 1 st, dc in next st, ch2, dc in next st, skip 1 st**, (2dc, ch2, 2dc) in 4-ch sp*, rep from * to * 2x and * to ** 1x, 2dc in same sp as first sts, ch2, join with ss to first st. Fasten off.
{6 sts, 1 2-ch sp on each side; 4 2-ch cnr sps}

R4: Attach B with stdg dc to any 2-ch cnr sp, *ch3, skip 3 sts, 3tr in 2-ch sp, ch3, skip 3 sts**, (dc, ch2, dc) in 2-ch sp*, rep from * to * 2x and * to ** 1x, dc in same sp as first st, ch1, join with dc to first st.
{5 sts, 2 3-ch sps on each side; 4 2-ch cnr sps}

R5: dc over joining dc, *skip 1 st, 3dc in 3-ch sp, skip 1 st, 5tr in next st, skip 1 st, 3dc in 3-ch sp, skip 1 st**, (dc, ch2, dc) in 2-ch sp*, rep from * to * 2x and * to ** 1x, dc in same sp as first st, ch2, join with ss to first st. Fasten off.
{13 sts on each side; 4 2-ch cnr sps}

R6: Attach C with stdg tr to any 2-ch cnr sp, tr in same sp, *ch5, skip 6 sts, dc in next st, ch5, skip 6 sts**, 3tr in 2-ch sp*, rep from * to * 2x and * to ** 1x, tr in same sp as first sts, join with ss to first st.
{1 st, 2 5-ch sps on each side; 4 3-st cnrs}

R7: dc in same st as ss, dc in next st, *6 dc in 5-ch sp, dc in next st, 6 dc in 5-ch sp**, dc in next 3 sts*, rep from * to * 2x and * to ** 1x, dc in next st, join with ss to first st. {64 sts}

R8: ch3 (stch), *2x [ch1, skip 1 st, htr in next st], 3x [ch1, skip 1 st, dc in next st], 2x [ch1, skip 1 st, htr in next st], ch1, skip 1 st**, (tr, ch3, tr) in next st*, rep from * to * 2x and * to ** 1x, tr in same st as first st, ch3, join with ss to 3rd ch of stch. Fasten off.
{9 sts, 8 1-ch sps on each side; 4 3-ch cnr sps}

R9: Attach D with stdg tr to any 3-ch cnr sp, ch1, tr in same sp, *8x [ch1, skip 1 st, tr in 1-ch sp], ch1, skip 1 st**, (2x [tr, ch1], tr) in 3-ch sp*, rep from * to * 2x and * to ** 1x, tr in same sp as first sts, ch1, join with ss to first st.
{10 sts, 11 1-ch sps on each side; 4 1-st cnrs}

R10: dc in same st as ss, *10x [dc in 1-ch sp, dc in next st], dc in 1-ch sp**, (dc, ch2, dc) in next st*, rep from * to * 2x and * to ** 1x, dc in same st as first st, ch1, join with dc to first st.
{23 sts on each side; 4 2-ch cnr sps}

R11: dc over joining dc, *dc in next 23 sts**, (dc, ch2, dc) in 2-ch sp*, rep from * to * 2x and * to ** 1x, dc in same sp as first st, ch2, join with ss to first st. Fasten off.
{25 sts on each side; 4 2-ch cnr sps}

ORESUND

A strait which forms the Danish–Swedish border
Φ 55.582381, λ 12.820093

Using A, begin with mc.

R1: ch3 (stch), tr, *ch2, 2tr*, rep from * to * 6x, ch2, join with ss to 3rd ch of stch. Fasten off.
{16 sts, 8 2-ch sps}

R2: Attach B with stdg tr to any 2-ch sp, 2tr in same sp, *skip 2 sts, 3tr in 2-ch sp*, rep from * to * 6x, join with ss to first st. {24 sts}

R3: ch3 (stch), tr in next 2 sts, *beginning around the st just worked, fptr2tog**, tr in st just worked, tr in next 2 sts*, rep from * to * 6x and * to ** 1x, join with ss to 3rd ch of stch. Fasten off. {32 sts}

R4: Attach C with stdg tr to middle st of any 3 sts between fp sts, ch1, tr in next st, ch1, *fptr around next st**, 3x [ch1, tr in next st], ch1*, rep from * to * 6x and * to ** 1x, ch1, tr in next st, ch1, join with ss to first st. {32 sts, 32 1-ch sps}

R5: ch3 (stch), 2tr in same st as ss, *skip 1-ch sp, 6x [dc in next st, dc in 1-ch sp], dc in next st, skip 1-ch sp**, (3tr, ch2, 3tr) in next st*, rep from * to * 2x and * to ** 1x, 3tr in same st as first sts, ch1, join with dc to 3rd ch of stch.
{19 sts on each side; 4 2-ch cnr sps}

R6: ch2 (stch), htr over joining dc, *htr in next 2 sts, 2htr in next st, skip 2 sts, dc in next 9 sts, skip 2 sts, 2htr in next st, htr in next 2 sts**, (2htr, ch2, 2htr) in 2-ch sp*, rep from * to * 2x and * to ** 1x, 2htr in same sp as first sts, ch2, join with ss to 2nd ch of stch. Fasten off.
{21 sts on each side; 4 2-ch cnr sps}

R7: Attach D with stdg tr to any 2-ch cnr sp, *7x [ch2, tr2tog over next 3 sts skipping the middle st], ch2**, (tr, ch2, tr) in 2-ch sp*, rep from * to * 2x and * to ** 1x, tr in same sp as first st, ch1, join with dc to first st.
{9 sts, 8 2-ch sps on each side; 4 2-ch cnr sps}

R8: dc over joining dc, *dc in next st, 7x [2dc in 2-ch sp, skip 1 st], 2dc in 2-ch sp, dc in next st**, (dc, ch2, dc) in 2-ch sp*, rep from * to * 2x and * to ** 1x, dc in same sp as first st, ch2, join with ss to first st. Fasten off.
{20 sts on each side; 4 2-ch cnr sps}

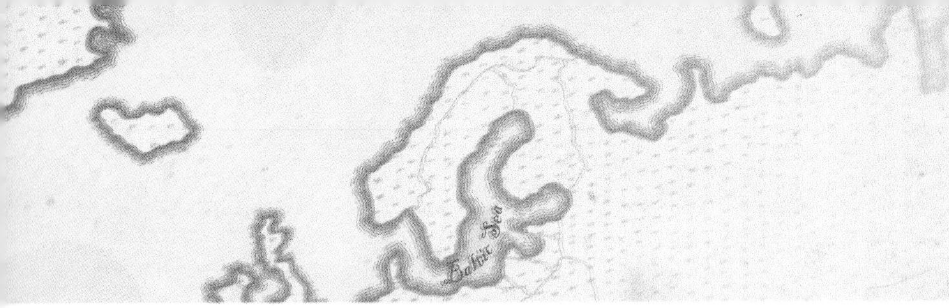

BALTIC

A marginal sea of the Atlantic Ocean
Φ 58.487953, λ 19.863281

Using A, attach yarn to hook with a slip knot, ch1, work all R1 sts into that ch.

R1: ch1, 8dc, join with ss to first st. {8 sts}

R2: ch3 (stch), tr in same st as ss, 2tr in next 7 sts, join with ss to 3rd ch of stch. {16 sts}

R3: Beginning in blo of next st, 8x [dc2tog in blo of next 2 sts], join with ss to first st. Fasten off. {8 sts}

R4: Attach B with stdg tr to any st, 4tr in same st, *ch2, skip 1 st**, 5tr in next st*, rep from * to * 2x and * to ** 1x, join with ss to first st. {2-ch sp on each side; 4 5-st cnrs}

R5: ch3 (stch), tr4tog over next 4 sts, *ch3, 5tr in 2-ch sp, ch3**, tr5tog over next 5 sts*, rep from * to * 2x and * to ** 1x, join with ss to top of tr4tog. {5 sts, 2 3-ch sps on each side; 4 1-st cnrs}

R6: ch3 (stch), *ch5, skip 3-ch sp, tr5tog over next 5 sts, ch5, skip 3-ch sp**, (tr, ch3, tr) in next st*, rep from * to * 2x and * to ** 1x, tr in same st as first st, ch3, join with ss to 3rd ch of stch. Fasten off. {3 sts, 2 5-ch sps on each side; 4 3-ch cnr sps}

R7: Attach C with stdg tr to any 3-ch cnr sp, 2tr in same sp, *ch2, skip 1 st, 5dtr over 5-ch sp of R6 and 3-ch sp of R5, ch2, htr in next st, ch2, 5dtr over 5-ch sp of R6 and 3-ch sp of R5, ch2, skip 1 st**, (3tr, ch2, 3tr) in 3-ch sp*, rep from * to * 2x and * to ** 1x, 3tr in same sp as first sts, ch1, join with dc to first st. {17 sts, 4 2-ch sps on each side; 4 2-ch cnr sps}

R8: dc over joining dc, *dc in next 3 sts, 2dc in 2-ch sp, dc2tog in first and 5th st of 5-dtr group, 2dc in 2-ch sp, dc in next st, 2dc in 2-ch sp, dc2tog in first and 5th st of 5-dtr group, 2dc in 2-ch sp, dc in next 3 sts**, (dc, ch2, dc) in 2-ch sp*, rep from * to * 2x and * to ** 1x, dc in same sp as first st, ch2, join with ss to first st. Fasten off. {19 sts on each side; 4 2-ch cnr sps}

R9: Attach D with stdg htr to any 2-ch cnr sp, *9x [ch1, skip 1 st, htr in next st], ch1, skip 1 st**, (htr, ch2, htr) in 2-ch sp*, rep from * to * 2x and * to ** 1x, htr in same sp as first st, ch1, join with dc to first st. {11 sts, 10 1-ch sps on each side; 4 2-ch cnr sps}

R10: dc over joining dc, *10x [dc in next st, dc in 1-ch sp], dc in next st**, (dc, ch2, dc) in 2-ch sp*, rep from * to * 2x and * to ** 1x, dc in same sp as first st, ch1, join with dc to first st. {23 sts on each side; 4 2-ch cnr sps}

R11: dc over joining dc, *dc in next 23 sts**, (dc, ch2, dc) in 2-ch sp*, rep from * to * 2x and * to ** 1x, dc in same sp as first st, ch2, join with ss to first st. Fasten off. {25 sts on each side; 4 2-ch cnr sps}

RIGA

A bay of the Baltic Sea between Latvia and Estonia
Φ 57.772713, λ 23.239034

Using A, attach yarn to hook with a slip knot, ch1, work all R1 sts into that ch.

R1: ch1, 12dc, join with ss to first st. {12 sts}

R2: dc in same st as ss, *ch1**, dc in next st*, rep from * to * 10x and * to ** 1x, join with ss to first st. {12 sts, 12 1-ch sps}

R3: ch3 (stch), *tr in 1-ch sp, tr around st just made**, tr in next st*, rep from * to * 10x and * to ** 1x, join with ss to 3rd ch of stch. Fasten off. {36 sts}

R4: Attach B with stdg dc to any st, dc in next 35 sts, join with ss to first st. {36 sts}

R5: ch3 (stch), *ch4, skip 2 sts**, tr in next st*, rep from * to * 10x and * to ** 1x, join with ss to 3rd ch of stch. {12 sts, 12 4-ch sps}

R6: dc in same st as ss, *4dc in 4-ch sp**, dc in next st*, rep from * to * 10x and * to ** 1x, join with ss to first st. Fasten off. {60 sts}

R7: Attach C with ss to any st, ch3 (stch), tr in next 59 sts, join with ss to 3rd ch of stch. Fasten off. {60 sts}

R8: Attach D with stdg dtr to any st above a tr of R5, 2x [ch1, dtr] in same st, *skip 3 sts, dc in next 8 sts, skip 3 sts**, (4x [dtr, ch1], dtr) in next st*, rep from * to * 2x and * to ** 1x, 2x [dtr, ch1] in same st as first sts, join with ss to first st.
{8 sts on each side; 4 (5 sts, 4 1-ch sps) cnrs}

R9: dc in same st as ss, *dc in 1-ch sp, dc in next st, dc in 1-ch sp, dc in next 10 sts, dc in 1-ch sp, dc in next st, dc in 1-ch sp**, (dc, ch2, dc) in next st*, rep from * to * 2x and * to ** 1x, dc in same st as first st, ch1, join with dc to first st.
{18 sts on each side; 4 2-ch cnr sps}

R10: dc over joining dc, *dc in next 18 sts**, (dc, ch2, dc) in 2-ch sp*, rep from * to * 2x and * to ** 1x, dc in same sp as first st, ch2, join with ss to first st. Fasten off.
{20 sts on each side; 4 2-ch cnr sps}

BISCAY

Located in the northeast Atlantic Ocean
and south of the Celtic Sea
Φ 45.051793, λ -3.598126

Using A, attach yarn to hook with a slip knot, ch1, work all R1 sts into that ch.

R1: ch1, 8dc, join with ss to first st. {8 sts}

R2: ch3 (stch), (tr, ch2, tr) in next 7 sts, tr in same st as first st, ch1, join with dc to 3rd ch of stch. {2 sts on each side; 8 2-ch cnr sps}

R3: ch3 (stch), tr over joining dc, *skip 2 sts**, (2tr, ch2, 2tr) in 2-ch sp*, rep from * to * 6x and * to ** 1x, 2tr in same sp as first sts, ch1, join with dc to 3rd ch of stch. {4 sts on each side; 8 2-ch cnr sps}

R4: dc over joining dc, *skip 1 st, dc in next 2 sts, skip 1 st**, (dc, ch1, dc) in 2-ch sp*, rep from * to * 6x and * to ** 1x, dc in same sp as first st, ch1, join with ss to first st. Fasten off. {4 sts on each side; 8 1-ch cnr sps}

R5: Attach B with stdg dc to any 1-ch sp, *ch5, skip 4 sts**, dc in 1-ch sp*, rep from * to * 6x and * to ** 1x, join with ss to first st. {8 sts, 8 5-ch sps}

R6: ch3 (stch), *7tr in 5-ch sp**, tr in next st*, rep from * to * 6x and * to ** 1x, join with ss to 3rd ch of stch. Fasten off. {64 sts}

R7: Attach C with stdg dtr to any single tr, *ch1, skip 1 st, hdtr in next st, ch1, skip 1 st, tr in next st, ch1, skip 1 st, htr in next st, ch1, skip 1 st, dc in next st, ch1, skip 1 st, htr in next st, ch1, skip 1 st, tr in next st, ch1, skip 1 st, hdtr in next st, ch1, skip 1 st**, (dtr, ch3, dtr) in next st*, rep from * to * 2x and * to ** 1x, dtr in same st as first st, ch3, join with ss to first st. Fasten off. {9 sts, 8 1-ch sps on each side; 4 3-ch cnr sps}

R8: Attach D with ss to any 3-ch cnr sp, ch3 (stch), tr in same sp, *8x [tr in next st, tr in 1-ch sp], tr in next st**, (2tr, ch2, 2tr) in 3-ch sp*, rep from * to * 2x and * to ** 1x, 2tr in same sp as first sts, ch2, join with ss to 3rd ch of stch. Fasten off. {21 sts on each side; 4 2-ch cnr sps}

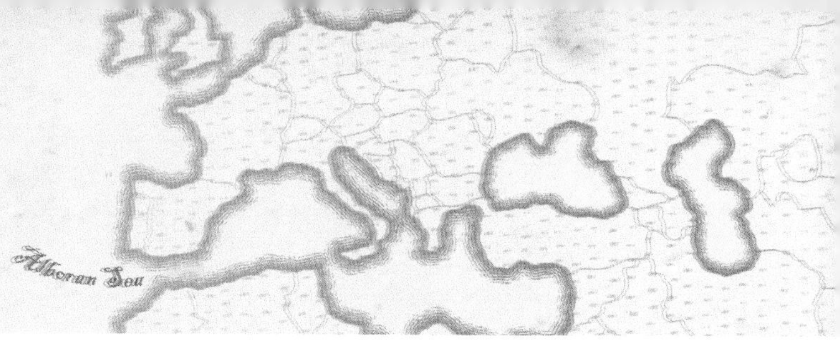

ALBORAN

The westernmost portion of the Mediterranean Sea
Φ 35.810686, λ -2.495316

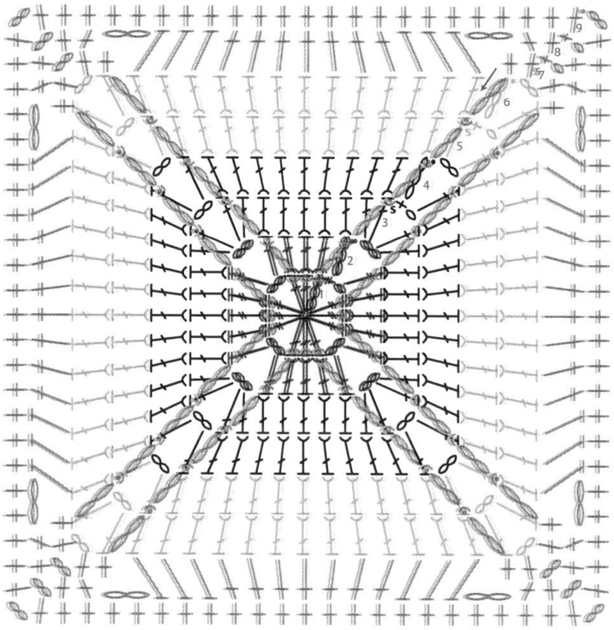

Using A, attach yarn to hook with a slip knot, ch1, work all R1 sts into that ch.

R1: ch3 (stch), 2tr, *ch2, 3tr*, rep from * to * 2x, ch1, join with dc to 3rd ch of stch.
{3 sts on each side; 4 2-ch cnr sps}

R2: ch3 (stch), *tr in blo of next 3 sts**, (tr, ch2, tr) in 2-ch sp*, rep from * to * 2x and * to ** 1x, tr in same sp as first st, ch2, join with ss to 3rd ch of stch. Fasten off.
{5 sts on each side; 4 2-ch cnr sps}

R3: Attach B with stdg tr to any 2-ch cnr sp, tr in same sp, *tr in blo of next 5 sts**, (2tr, ch2, 2tr) in 2-ch sp*, rep from * to * 2x and * to ** 1x, 2tr in same sp as first sts, ch1, join with dc to first st. {9 sts on each side; 4 2-ch cnr sps}

R4: ch3 (stch), *tr in blo of next 9 sts**, (tr, ch2, tr) in 2-ch sp*, rep from * to * 2x and * to ** 1x, tr in same sp as first st, ch2, join with ss to 3rd ch of stch. Fasten off.
{11 sts on each side; 4 2-ch cnr sps}

R5: Attach C with stdg tr to any 2-ch cnr sp, *tr in blo of next 11 sts**, (tr, ch2, tr) in 2-ch sp*, rep from * to * 2x and * to ** 1x, tr in same sp as first st, ch1, join with dc to first st.
{13 sts on each side; 4 2-ch cnr sps}

R6: ch3 (stch), *tr in blo of next 13 sts**, (tr, ch2, tr) in 2-ch sp*, rep from * to * 2x and * to ** 1x, tr in same sp as first st, ch2, join with ss to 3rd ch of stch. Fasten off.
{15 sts on each side; 4 2-ch cnr sps}

R7: Attach D with stdg dc to any 2-ch cnr sp, *dc in next st, 5x [ch2, ss in flo of first st of round below], ss in flo of next 2 sts of the side of R1, 4x [ch2, ss in flo of last st of the side of the round above], ch2, dc in last st of R6**, (dc, ch2, dc) in 2-ch sp*, rep from * to * 2x and * to ** 1x, dc in same sp as first st, ch1, join with dc to first st.
{4 sts in R7, 10 2-ch sps, 11 ss on each side; 4 2-ch cnr sps}

R8: dc over joining dc, *dc in next st, ch2, skip 1 st, htr in next 3 sts of R6, dc in next 7 sts of R6, htr in next 3 sts of R6, ch2, skip 1 st, dc in next st**, (dc, ch2, dc) in 2-ch sp*, rep from * to * 2x and * to ** 1x, dc in same sp as first st, ch1, join with dc to first st.
{17 sts, 2 2-ch sps on each side; 4 2-ch cnr sps}

R9: dc over joining dc, *dc in next 2 sts, 2dc in 2-ch sp, dc in next 13 sts, 2dc in 2-ch sp, dc in next 2 sts**, (dc, ch2, dc) in 2-ch sp*, rep from * to * 2x and * to ** 1x, dc in same sp as first st, ch2, join with ss to first st. Fasten off.
{23 sts on each side; 4 2-ch cnr sps}

CATALAN

A body of water in the Mediterranean Sea
near the Balearic Islands
Φ 41.003117, λ 2.099626

Using A, begin with mc.

R1: ch3 (stch), tr, *ch3, 2tr*, rep from * to * 6x, ch1, join with htr to 3rd ch of stch. {16 sts, 8 3-ch sps}

R2: ch3 (stch), 3tr over joining htr, *skip (2 sts, 3-ch sp and 2 sts)**, (4tr, ch2, 4tr) in 3-ch sp*, rep from * to * 2x and * to ** 1x, 4tr in same sp as first sts, ch2, join with ss to 3rd ch of stch. Fasten off. {8 sts on each side; 4 2-ch cnr sps}

R3: Attach B with stdg dc to any 2-ch cnr sp, *dc in next 4 sts of R2, (4tr, ch2, 4tr) in 3-ch sp of R1 below, dc in next 4 sts of R2**, (dc, ch2, dc) in 2-ch sp*, rep from * to * 2x and * to ** 1x, dc in same sp as first st, ch1, join with dc to first st. {18 sts, 1 2-ch sp on each side; 4 2-ch cnr sps}

R4: ch3 (stch), *tr in next 5 sts, skip (4tr, 2-ch sp and 4tr), tr in next 5 sts**, (tr, ch2, tr) in 2-ch sp*, rep from * to * 2x and * to ** 1x, tr in same sp as first st, ch1, join with dc to 3rd ch of stch. {12 sts on each side; 4 2-ch cnr sps}

R5: dc over joining dc, *dc in next 6 sts, dc in 2-ch sp of R3 below, dc in next 6 sts**, (dc, ch2, dc) in 2-ch sp*, rep from * to * 2x and * to ** 1x, dc in same sp as first st, ch1, join with dc to first st. {15 sts on each side; 4 2-ch cnr sps}

R6: ch3 (stch), *7x [ch1, skip 1 st, tr in next st], ch1, skip 1 st**, (tr, ch2, tr) in 2-ch sp*, rep from * to * 2x and * to ** 1x, tr in same sp as first st, ch2, join with ss to 3rd ch of stch. Fasten off. {9 sts, 8 1-ch sps on each side; 4 2-ch cnr sps}

R7: Attach C with stdg dc to any 2-ch cnr sp, *8x [dc in next st, spike dc in next st of R5 below], dc in next st**, (dc, ch2, dc) in 2-ch sp*, rep from * to * 2x and * to ** 1x, dc in same sp as first st, ch1, join with dc to first st. {19 sts on each side; 4 2-ch cnr sps}

R8: ch2 (stch), *9x [ch1, skip 1 st, htr in next st], ch1, skip 1 st**, (htr, ch2, htr) in 2-ch sp*, rep from * to * 2x and * to ** 1x, htr in same sp as first st, ch2, join with ss to 2nd ch of stch. Fasten off. {11 sts, 10 1-ch sps on each side; 4 2-ch cnr sps}

R9: Attach D with stdg dc to any 2-ch cnr sp, *10x [dc in next st, spike dc in next st of R7 below], dc in next st**, (dc, ch2, dc) in 2-ch sp*, rep from * to * 2x and * to ** 1x, dc in same sp as first st, ch2, join with ss to first st. Fasten off. {23 sts on each side; 4 2-ch cnr sps}

SARDINIA

Located in the Mediterranean Sea
Φ 40.064620, λ 6.089118

☆ *2χ = skip 1 st, tr in next st, tr in skipped st.*
3χ = skip 2 sts, tr in next st, tr in 2nd skipped st, tr in first skipped st.
4χ = skip 3 sts, tr in next st, tr in 3rd skipped st, tr in 2nd skipped st, tr in first skipped st.

Using A, attach yarn to hook with a slip knot, ch1, work all R1 sts into that ch.

R1: ch3 (stch), 2tr, *ch2, 3tr*, rep from * to * 2x, ch1, join with dc to 3rd ch of stch.
{12 sts, 4 2-ch cnr sps}

R2: ch3 (stch), tr over joining dc, *3χ**, (2tr, ch2, 2tr) in 2-ch sp*, rep from * to * 2x and * to ** 1x, 2tr in same sp as first sts, ch2, join with ss to 3rd ch of stch. Fasten off.
{7 sts on each side; 4 2-ch cnr sps}

R3: Attach B with stdg tr to any 2-ch cnr sp, tr in same sp, *3χ, skip 1 st, 3χ**, (2tr, ch2, 2tr) in 2-ch sp*, rep from * to * 2x and * to ** 1x, 2tr in same sp as first sts, ch1, join with dc to first st.
{10 sts on each side; 4 2-ch cnr sps}

R4: ch3 (stch), tr over joining dc, *3χ, 4χ, 3χ**, (2tr, ch2, 2tr) in 2-ch sp*, rep from * to * 2x and * to ** 1x, 2tr in same sp as first sts, ch2, join with ss to 3rd ch of stch. Fasten off.
{14 sts on each side; 4 2-ch cnr sps}

R5: Attach C with stdg tr to any 2-ch cnr sp, tr in same sp, *2x 3χ, 2χ, 2x 3χ**, (2tr, ch2, 2tr) in 2-ch sp*, rep from * to * 2x and * to ** 1x, 2tr in same sp as first sts, ch1, join with dc to first st.
{18 sts on each side; 4 2-ch cnr sps}

R6: ch3 (stch), tr over joining dc, *6x 3χ**, (2tr, ch2, 2tr) in 2-ch sp*, rep from * to * 2x and * to ** 1x, 2tr in same sp as first sts, ch2, join with ss to 3rd ch of stch. Fasten off.
{22 sts on each side; 4 2-ch cnr sps}

R7: Attach D with stdg dc to any 2-ch cnr sp, *dc in next 22 sts**, (dc, ch2, dc) in 2-ch sp*, rep from * to * 2x and * to ** 1x, dc in same sp as first st, ch2, join with ss to first st. Fasten off.
{24 sts on each side; 4 2-ch cnr sps}

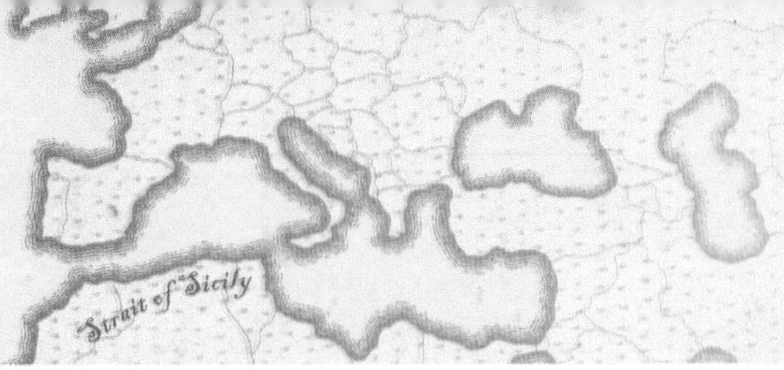

SICILY

The strait between Sicily and Tunisia
Φ 37.333330, λ 11.333330

Using A, begin with mc.

R1: ch1, *dc, ch3, 3dtr, ch3*, rep from * to * 3x, join with ss to first st. Fasten off.
{3 sts, 2 3-ch sps on each side; 4 1-st cnrs}

R2: Attach B with stdg dtr to any dc, *ch2, dc in 3-ch sp, dc in next 3 sts, dc in 3-ch sp, ch2**, dtr in next st*, rep from * to * 2x and * to ** 1x, join with ss to first st.
{5 sts, 2 2-ch sps on each side; 4 1-st cnrs}

R3: dc in same st as ss, *2dc in 2-ch sp, dc in next st, ch3, dtr in next 3 sts, ch3, dc in next st, 2dc in 2-ch sp**, (dc, ch2, dc) in next st*, rep from * to * 2x and * to ** 1x, dc in same st as first st, ch2, join with ss to first st. Fasten off.
{11 sts, 2 3-ch sps on each side; 4 2-ch cnr sps}

R4: Attach C with stdg dtr to any 2-ch cnr sp, ch1, dtr in same sp, *ch2, skip 4 sts, dc in 3-ch sp, dc in next 3 sts, dc in 3-ch sp, ch2, skip 4 sts**, (2x [dtr, ch1], dtr) in 2-ch sp*, rep from * to * 2x and * to ** 1x, dtr in same sp as first sts, ch1, join with ss to first st.
{7 sts, 2 2-ch sps, 2 1-ch sps on each side; 4 1-st cnrs}

R5: dc in same st as ss, *dc in 1-ch sp, dc in next st, 2dc in 2-ch sp, dc in next st, ch3, dtr in next 3 sts, ch3, dc in next st, 2dc in 2-ch sp, dc in next st, dc in 1-ch sp**, (dc, ch2, dc) in next st*, rep from * to * 2x and * to ** 1x, dc in same st as first st, ch2, join with ss to first st. Fasten off.
{15 sts, 2 3-ch sps on each side; 4 2-ch cnr sps}

R6: Attach D with stdg dtr to any 2-ch cnr sp, ch1, dtr in same sp, *ch1, skip 1 st, dtr in next st, ch3, skip 4 sts, dc in 3-ch sp, dc in next 3 sts, dc in 3-ch sp, ch3, skip 4 sts, dtr in next st, ch1, skip 1 st**, (2x [dtr, ch1], dtr) in 2-ch sp*, rep from * to * 2x and * to ** 1x, dtr in same sp as first sts, ch1, join with ss to first st.
{9 sts, 2 3-ch sps, 4 1-ch sps on each side; 4 1-st cnrs}

R7: dc in same st as ss, *2x [dc in 1-ch sp, dc in next st], 3dc in 3-ch sp, dc in next 5 sts, 3dc in 3-ch sp, 2x [dc in next st, dc in 1-ch sp]**, (dc, ch2, dc) in next st*, rep from * to * 2x and * to ** 1x, dc in same st as first st, ch2, join with ss to first st. Fasten off. {21 sts on each side; 4 2-ch cnr sps}

IONIAN

Located in the Mediterranean Sea, south of the Adriatic Sea
Φ 37.708161, λ 18.700319

Using A, attach yarn to hook with a slip knot, ch1, work all R1 sts into that ch.

R1: ch1, 8dc, join with ss to first st. {8 sts}

R2: ch3 (stch), *ch1, tr in next st*, rep from * to * 6x, ch1, join with ss to 3rd ch of stch. {8 sts, 8 1-ch sps}

R3: dc in same st as ss, *ch2, skip 1-ch sp, fptr around next st, ch2**, dc in same st fp st was worked around*, rep from * to * 6x and * to ** 1x, join with ss to first st. {16 sts, 16 2-ch sps}

R4: dc in same st as ss, *fptr around fp st slightly to the right below, dc in 2-ch sp, skip 1 st, dc in 2-ch sp**, dc in next st*, rep from * to * 6x and * to ** 1x, join with ss to first st. Fasten off. {32 sts}

R5: Attach B with ss to any st before a fp st, (ch3, puff, ch3, ss) in same st, *dc in next 3 sts**, (ss, ch3, puff, ch3, ss) in next st*, rep from * to * 6x and * to ** 1x, join with ss to ss attaching B. Fasten off. {32 sts, 16 3-ch sps}

R6: Attach C with stdg tr to any 3-ch sp before puff, *ch3, skip 1 st, tr in 3-ch sp, dtr in blo of next 3 sts, tr in 3-ch sp, ch3, skip 1 st, tr in 3-ch sp**, ch5, skip 3 sts, tr in 3-ch sp*, rep from * to * 2x and * to ** 1x, ch1, join with tr to first st. {7 sts, 2 3-ch sps on each side; 4 5-ch cnr sps}

R7: ch3 (stch), 2tr over joining tr, *tr in next st, (2htr, dc) in 3-ch sp, dc in next st, fphtr around next 3 sts, dc in next st, (dc, 2htr) in 3-ch sp, tr in next st**, (3tr, ch2, 3tr) in 5-ch sp*, rep from * to * 2x and * to ** 1x, 3tr in same sp as first sts, ch1, join with dc to 3rd ch of stch. Fasten off. {19 sts on each side; 4 2-ch cnr sps}

R8: Attach D with ss to any 2-ch cnr sp, ch3 (stch), *tr in next 8 sts, hdtr in next 3 sts of R6 behind R7, tr in next 8 sts**, (tr, ch2, tr) in 2-ch sp*, rep from * to * 2x and * to ** 1x, tr in same sp as first st, ch2, join with ss to 3rd ch of stch. Fasten off. {21 sts on each side; 4 2-ch cnr sps}

SIDRA

Located in the Mediterranean Sea
on the northern coast of Libya
Φ 31.877558, λ 18.387394

☆ *do not use false st at start of R2.*

Using A, attach yarn to hook with a slip knot, ch1, work all R1 sts into that ch.

R1: ch1, 12dc, join with ss to first st. {12 sts}

R2: ch3 (stch), tr in same st as ss, 2tr in next 11 sts, join with inv join to first true tr. Fasten off. {24 sts}

R3: Attach B with bpss to any st, ch3 (stch), bphdtr around next 23 sts, join with ss to 3rd ch of stch. Fasten off. {24 sts}

R4: Attach C with stdg dtr to any st, 4dtr in same st, *ch2, skip 1 st**, 5dtr in next st*, rep from * to * 10x and * to ** 1x, join with ss to first st. {60 sts, 12 2-ch sps}

R5: *dc in both 2-ch sps on either side of the next 5 sts at the same time, dc in 2-ch sp, dc in next 5 sts, dc in 2-ch sp*, rep from * to * 5x, join with ss to first st. Fasten off. {48 sts}

R6: Attach D with stdg dtr to any dc that gathered 5 sts together, hdtr in same st, *tr in next st, htr in next st, dc in next 7 sts, htr in next st, tr in next st**, (hdtr, dtr, hdtr) in next st*, rep from * to * 2x and * to ** 1x, hdtr in same st as first sts, join with ss to first st. {11 sts on each side; 4 3-st cnrs}

R7: ch3 (stch), 2tr in same st as ss, *tr in next 13 sts**, (2tr, hdtr, 2tr) in next st*, rep from * to * 2x and * to ** 1x, 2tr in same st as first sts, join with ss to 3rd ch of stch. {13 sts on each side; 4 5-st cnrs}

R8: dc in same st as ss, *dc in next 17 sts**, (dc, ch2, dc) in next st*, rep from * to * 2x and * to ** 1x, dc in same st as first st, ch1, join with dc to first st. {19 sts on each side; 4 2-ch cnr sps}

R9: dc over joining dc, *dc in next 19 sts**, (dc, ch2, dc) in 2-ch sp*, rep from * to * 2x and * to ** 1x, dc in same sp as first st, ch2, join with ss to first st. Fasten off. {21 sts on each side; 4 2-ch cnr sps}

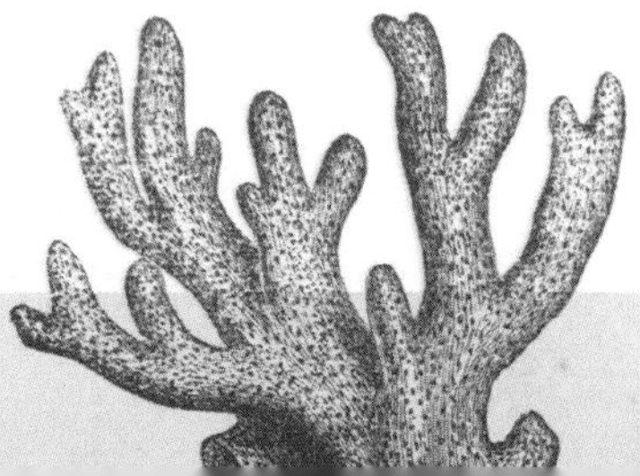

LEVANTINE

Bordered by the Aegean Sea in the northwest
Φ 33.812015, λ 31.666159

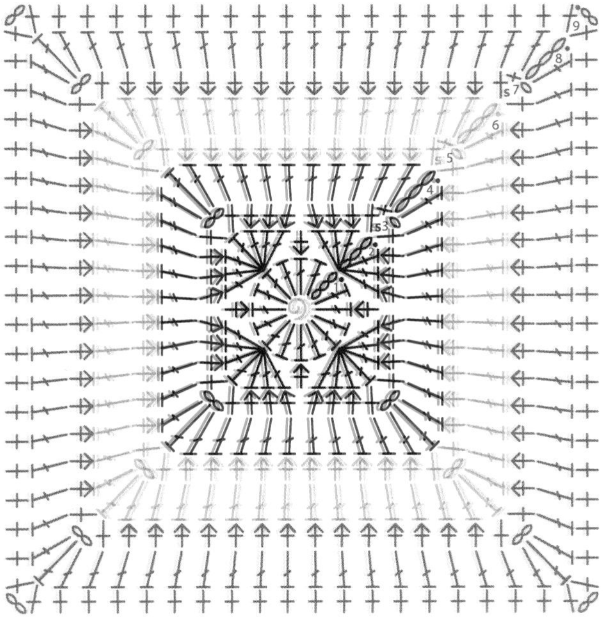

Using A, begin with mc.

R1: ch3 (stch), 15tr, join with ss to 3rd ch of stch. {16 sts}

R2: ch3 (stch), 3tr in same st as ss, *skip 1 st, dc in lbv of next st, skip 1 st**, 7tr in next st*, rep from * to * 2x and * to ** 1x, 3tr in same st as first sts, join with ss to 3rd ch of stch. Fasten off. {1 st on each side; 4 7-st cnrs}

R3: Attach B with stdg dc to middle st of any 7-st group, *dc in lbv of next 3 sts, skip 1 st, dc in lbv of next 3 sts**, (dc, ch2, dc) in next st*, rep from * to * 2x and * to ** 1x, dc in same st as first st, ch1, join with dc to first st.
{8 sts on each side; 4 2-ch cnr sps}

R4: ch3 (stch), tr over joining dc, *tr in next 8 sts**, 3tr in 2-ch sp*, rep from * to * 2x and * to ** 1x, tr in same sp as first sts, join with ss to 3rd ch of stch. Fasten off.
{8 sts on each side; 4 3-st cnrs}

R5: Attach C with stdg dc to middle st of any 3-st group, *dc in lbv of next 10 sts**, (dc, ch2, dc) in next st*, rep from * to * 2x and * to ** 1x, dc in same st as first st, ch1, join with dc to first st. {12 sts on each side; 4 2-ch cnr sps}

R6: ch3 (stch), tr over joining dc, *tr in next 12 sts**, 3tr in 2-ch sp*, rep from * to * 2x and * to ** 1x, tr in same sp as first sts, join with ss to 3rd ch of stch. Fasten off.
{12 sts on each side; 4 3-st cnrs}

R7: Attach D with stdg dc to middle st of any 3-st group, *dc in lbv of next 14 sts**, (dc, ch2, dc) next st*, rep from * to * 2x and * to ** 1x, dc in same st as first st, ch1, join with dc to first st.
{16 sts on each side; 4 2-ch cnr sps}

R8: ch3 (stch), tr over joining dc, *tr in next 16 sts**, 3tr in 2-ch sp*, rep from * to * 2x and * to ** 1x, tr in same sp as first sts, join with ss to 3rd ch of stch.
{16 sts on each side; 4 3-st cnrs}

R9: dc in same st as ss, *dc in next 18 sts**, (dc, ch2, dc) in next st*, rep from * to * 2x and * to ** 1x, dc in same st as first st, ch2, join with ss to first st. Fasten off.
{20 sts on each side; 4 2-ch cnr sps}

ADRIATIC

The northernmost arm of the Mediterranean Sea

Φ 42.533654, λ 16.059664

★ *triangle = ch4, dc in 2nd ch from hook, htr in 3rd ch, tr in 4th ch.*

Using A, begin with mc.

R1: ch3 (stch), 15tr, join with ss to 3rd ch of stch. {16 sts}

R2: *triangle, skip 3 sts**, ss in next st*, rep from * to * 2x and * to ** 1x, join with ss to ss join of R1. Fasten off. {4 triangles, 4 ss}

R3: Attach B with ss to any ss, *triangle, ch3, triangle, skip triangle of R2**, ss into ss between R2 triangles*, rep from * to * 2x and * to ** 1x, join with ss to first ss. Fasten off. {8 triangles, 4 3-ch sps}

R4: Attach C with stdg dtr to any ss, *ch5, skip triangle, dc in 3-ch sp, ch5, skip triangle**, dtr in ss between R3 triangles*, rep from * to * 2x and * to ** 1x, join with ss to first st. {8 sts, 8 5-ch sps}

R5: dc in same st as ss, *5dc in 5-ch sp, dc in next st, 5dc in 5-ch sp**, (dc, ch2, dc) in next st*, rep from * to * 2x and * to ** 1x, dc in same st as first st, ch1, join with dc to first st. {13 sts on each side; 4 2-ch cnr sps}

R6: *2x [triangle, skip 2 sts, ss in next st], triangle, skip 1 st, ss in next st, triangle, skip 2 sts, ss in next st, triangle, skip 2 sts**, ss in 2-ch sp*, rep from * to * 2x and * to ** 1x, join with ss in 2-ch cnr sp. Fasten off. {5 triangles, 4 ss on each side; 4 ss cnrs}

R7: Attach D with stdg dtr to any ss in a 2-ch sp, *4x [ch3, skip triangle, hdtr in ss], ch3, skip triangle**, (dtr, ch2, dtr) in next ss*, rep from * to * 2x and * to ** 1x, dtr in same st as first st, ch1, join with dc to first st. {6 sts, 5 3-ch sps on each side; 4 2-ch cnr sps}

R8: dc over joining dc, *5x [dc in next st, 2dc in 3-ch sp], dc in next st**, (dc, ch2, dc) in 2-ch sp*, rep from * to * 2x and * to ** 1x, dc in same sp as first st, ch1, join with dc to first st. {18 sts on each side; 4 2-ch cnr sps}

R9: dc over joining dc, *dc in next 18 sts**, (dc, ch2, dc) in 2-ch sp*, rep from * to * 2x and * to ** 1x, dc in same sp as first st, ch2, join with ss to first st. Fasten off. {20 sts on each side; 4 2-ch cnr sps}

THRACIAN

Northernmost point of the Aegean Sea
Φ 40.250000, λ 24.416700

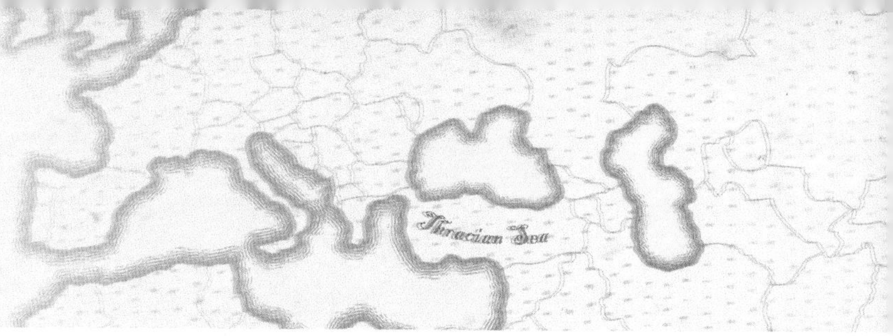

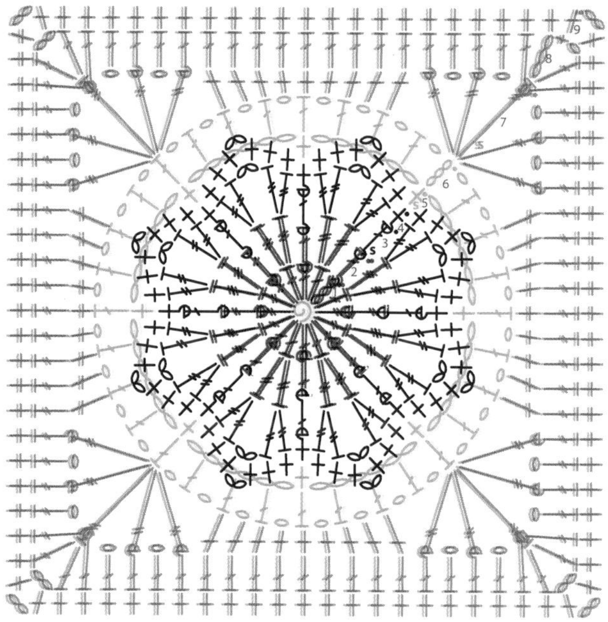

Using A, begin with mc.

R1: ch3 (stch), 15tr, join with ss to 3rd ch of stch. {16 sts}

R2: fptr around same st as ss, *2dtr in next st**, fptr around next st*, rep from * to * 6x and * to ** 1x, join with ss to first st. Fasten off. {24 sts}

R3: Attach B with stdg fptr around any fp st, *2dtr in next st, ch2, 2dtr in next st**, fptr around next st*, rep from * to * 6x and * to ** 1x, join with ss to first st. {40 sts, 8 2-ch sps}

R4: fpdc around same st as ss, *dc in next 2 sts, (dc, ch2, dc) in 2-ch sp, dc in next 2 sts**, fpdc around next st*, rep from * to * 6x and * to ** 1x, join with ss to first st. Fasten off.
{56 sts, 8 2-ch sps}

R5: Attach C with stdg dc to any fp st, *ch6, skip (3 sts, 2-ch sp and 3 sts)**, dc in next st*, rep from * to * 6x and * to ** 1x, join with ss to first st. {8 sts, 8 6-ch sps}

R6: ch3 (stch), *3x [ch1, tr] in 6-ch sp, ch1**, tr in next st*, rep from * to * 6x and * to ** 1x, join with ss to 3rd ch of stch. Fasten off.
{32 sts, 32 1-ch sps}

R7: Attach D with stdg dtr to any st above a fp st, 2x [ch1, dtr] in same st, *skip (1-ch sp, 1 st and 1-ch sp), 4x [dc in next st, dc in 1-ch sp], dc in next st, skip (1-ch sp, 1 st and 1-ch sp)**, (4x [dtr, ch1], dtr) in next st*, rep from * to * 2x and * to ** 1x, 2x [dtr, ch1] in same st as first sts, join with ss to first st.
{13 sts, 4 1-ch sps on each side; 4 1-st cnrs}

R8: ch3 (stch), fptr around same st as ss, *2x [tr in 1-ch sp, fptr around next st], tr in next 9 sts, 2x [fptr around next st, tr in 1-ch sp], fptr around next st**, (tr, ch2, tr) in same st fp st was worked around, fptr around same st*, rep from * to * 2x and * to ** 1x, tr in same st as first st, ch1, join with dc to 3rd ch of stch.
{21 sts on each side, 4 2-ch cnr sps}

R9: dc over joining dc, *dc in next 21 sts**, (dc, ch2, dc) in 2-ch sp*, rep from * to * 2x and * to ** 1x, dc in same sp as first st, ch2, join with ss to first st. Fasten off.
{23 sts on each side; 4 2-ch cnr sps}

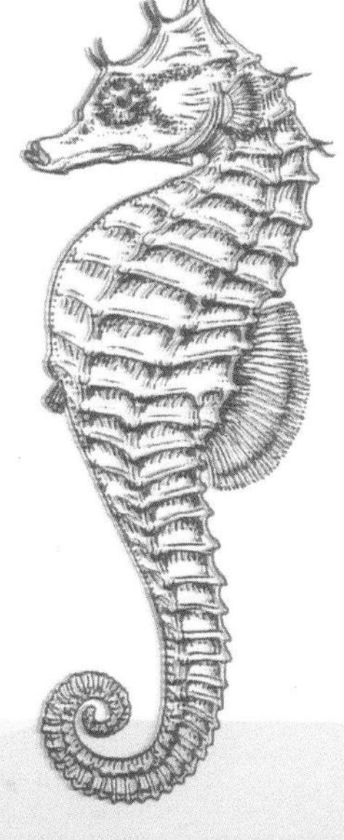

AEGEAN

Located between the mainlands of Greece and Turkey
Φ 39.019184, λ -25.268555

Using A, attach yarn to hook with a slip knot, ch1, work all R1 sts into that ch.

R1: ch3 (stch), 11tr, join with ss to 3rd ch of stch. Fasten off. {12 sts}

R2: Attach B with a stdg dc to any st, *ch3, skip 1 st**, dc in next st*, rep from * to * 4x and * to ** 1x, join with ss to first st. {6 sts, 6 3-ch sps}

R3: ch3 (stch), *ch2, dc in 3-ch sp, ch2**, tr in next st*, rep from * to * 4x and * to ** 1x, join with ss to 3rd ch of stch. {12 sts, 12 2-ch sps}

R4: ch3 (stch), *(htr, dc) in 2-ch sp, skip 1 st, (dc, htr) in 2-ch sp**, (tr, ch2, tr) in next st*, rep from * to * 4x and * to ** 1x, tr in same st as first st, ch2, join with ss to 3rd ch of stch. Fasten off.
{36 sts, 6 2-ch sps}

R5: Attach C with a stdg dc to any 2-ch sp, *ch8, skip 6 sts**, dc in 2-ch sp*, rep from * to * 4x and * to ** 1x, join with ss to first st.
{6 sts, 6 8-ch sps}

R6: ch3 (stch), *9tr in 8-ch sp**, tr in next st*, rep from * to * 4x and * to ** 1x, join with ss to 3rd ch of stch. Fasten off. {60 sts}

R7: Attach D with a stdg hdtr to a st in a st above a star point, hdtr in same st, *tr in next 2 sts, htr in next 3 sts, dc in next 4 sts, htr in next 3 sts, tr in next 2 sts**, (2hdtr, ch2, 2hdtr) in next st*, rep from * to * 2x and * to ** 1x, 2hdtr in same st as first sts, ch1, join with dc to first st.
{18 sts on each side; 4 2-ch cnr sps}

R8: dc over joining dc, *dc in next 18 sts**, (dc, ch2, dc) in 2-ch sp*, rep from * to * 2x and * to ** 1x, dc in same sp as first st, ch1, join with dc to first st. {20 sts on each side; 4 2-ch cnr sps}

R9: dc over joining dc, *dc in next 20 sts**, (dc, ch2, dc) in 2-ch sp*, rep from * to * 2x and * to ** 1x, dc in same sp as first st, ch1, join with dc to first st. {22 sts on each side; 4 2-ch cnr sps}

R10: dc over joining dc, *dc in next 22 sts**, (dc, ch2, dc) in 2-ch sp*, rep from * to * 2x and * to ** 1x, dc in same sp as first st, ch2, join with ss to first st. Fasten off.
{24 sts on each side; 4 2-ch cnr sps}

MARMARA

An inland sea, entirely within the borders of Turkey
Φ 40.673972, λ 28.313581

Using A, attach yarn to hook with a slip knot, ch1, work all R1 sts into that ch.

R1: ch3 (stch), *ch2, tr*, rep from * to * 6x, ch2, join with ss to 3rd ch of stch. {8 sts, 8 2-ch sps}

R2: dc in same st as ss, *(htr, tr, ch2, tr, htr) in 2-ch sp**, dc in next st*, rep from * to * 6x and * to ** 1x, join with ss to first st. Fasten off. {40 sts, 8 2-ch sps}

R3: Attach B with stdg bpdc around any R1 st, *ch2, bpdc around next R1 st*, rep from * to * 6x, ch1, join with dc to first st. {8 sts, 8 2-ch sps}

R4: dc over joining dc, *5tr in next st**, dc in 2-ch sp*, rep from * to * 6x and * to ** 1x, join with ss to first st. {48 sts}

R5: dc in same st as ss, *ch3, skip 2 sts**, dc in next st*, rep from * to * 14x and * to ** 1x, join with ss to first st. Fasten off. {16 sts, 16 3-ch sps}

R6: Attach C with stdg tr to any st of R5 between 5-st groups of R4, *(tr, htr) in 3-ch sp, dc in next st, (htr, tr) in 3-ch sp**, tr in next st*, rep from * to * 6x and * to ** 1x, join with ss to first st. {48 sts}

R7: dc in same st as ss, dc in next 47 sts, join with ss to first st. Fasten off. {48 sts}

R8: Attach D with stdg dtr to any st, *ch1, skip 1 st, tr in next st, ch1, skip 1 st, htr in next st, ch1, skip 1 st, dc in next st, ch1, skip 1 st, htr in next st, ch1, skip 1 st, tr in next st, ch1, skip 1 st**, (dtr, ch3, dtr) in next st*, rep from * to * 2x and * to ** 1x, dtr in same st as first st, ch1, join with htr to first st.
{7 sts, 6 1-ch sps on each side; 4 3-ch cnr sps}

R9: 2dc over joining htr, *6x [dc in next st, dc in 1-ch sp], dc in next st**, (2dc, ch2, 2dc) in 3-ch sp*, rep from * to * 2x and * to ** 1x, 2dc in same sp as first sts, ch1, join with dc to first st.
{17 sts on each side; 4 2-ch cnr sps}

R10: ch3 (stch), tr over joining dc, *3x [ch2, skip 2 sts, tr in next 3 sts], ch2, skip 2 sts**, (2tr, ch2, 2tr) in 2-ch sp*, rep from * to * 2x and * to ** 1x, 2tr in same sp as first sts, ch1, join with dc to 3rd ch of stch.
{13 sts, 4 2-ch sps on each side; 4 2-ch cnr sps}

R11: dc over joining dc, *dc in next 2 sts, 3x [2dc in 2-ch sp, dc in next 3 sts], 2dc in 2-ch sp, dc in next 2 sts**, (dc, ch2, dc) in 2-ch sp*, rep from * to * 2x and * to ** 1x, dc in same sp as first st, ch2, join with ss to first st. Fasten off.
{23 sts on each side; 4 2-ch cnr sps}

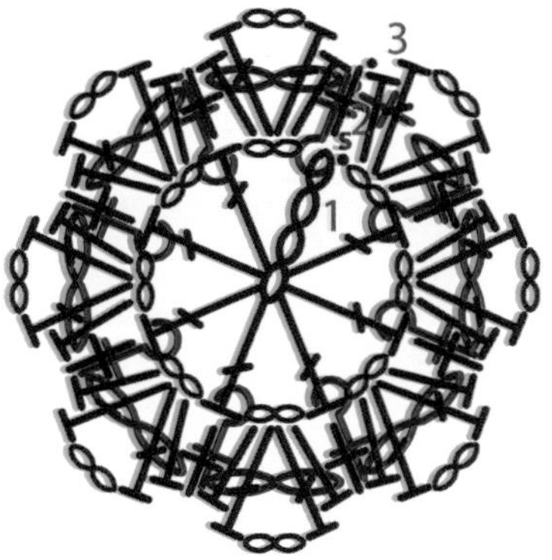

AZOV

Located in Eastern Europe
Φ 46.067133, λ 36.750350

Using A, ch8, join last ch to first with a ss over the top 2 strands of the first ch.

R1: ch3 (stch), tr in same ch as ss, *ch2, 2tr in next ch*, rep from * to * 6x, ch1, join with dc to 3rd ch of stch. Fasten off. {16 sts, 8 2-ch sps}

R2: Attach B with a stdg tr to any 2-ch sp, 2tr in same sp, *skip 2 sts**, 5tr in 2-ch sp*, rep from * to * 6x and * to ** 1x, 2tr in same sp as first sts, join with ss to first st. {40 sts}

R3: ch3 (stch), *ch1, skip 1 st**, tr in next st*, rep from * to * 18x and * to ** 1x, join with ss to 3rd ch of stch. Fasten off. {20 sts, 20 1-ch sps}

R4: Attach C with a stdg dc to any st, *spike dc in skipped st of R2 below**, dc in next st*, rep from * to * 18x and * to ** 1x, join with ss to first st. {40 sts}

R5: ch3 (stch), *ch2, skip 1 st**, tr in next st*, rep from * to * 18x and * to ** 1x, join with ss to 3rd ch of stch. {20 sts, 20 2-ch sps}

R6: dc in same st as ss, *2dc in 2-ch sp**, dc in next st*, rep from * to * 18x and * to ** 1x, join with ss to first st. {60 sts}

R7: ch3 (stch), ch1, tr in same st as ss, *ch1, skip 1 st, tr in next st, ch1, skip 1 st, htr in next st, ch1, skip 1 st, dc in next st, ch2, skip 2 sts, dc in next st, ch1, skip 1 st, htr in next st, ch1, skip 1 st, tr in next st, ch1, skip 1 st**, (2x [tr, ch1], tr) in next st*, rep from * to * 2x and * to ** 1x, tr in same st as first sts, ch1, join with ss to 3rd ch of stch. Fasten off.
{8 sts, 1 2-ch sp, 8 1-ch sps on each side; 4 1-st cnrs}

R8: Attach D with stdg dc to any 1-st cnr, *spike dc in same st R7 cnr st is worked into, 3x [dc in next st, spike dc in skipped st of R6 below], dc in next st, spike dc in next 2 skipped sts of R6 below, 3x [dc in next st, spike dc in skipped st of R6 below], dc in next st, spike dc in same st R7 cnr st is worked into**, (dc, ch2, dc) in next st*, rep from * to * 2x and * to ** 1x, dc in same st as first st, ch1, join with dc to first st.
{20 sts on each side; 4 2-ch cnr sps}

R9: ch3 (stch), *tr in next 20 sts**, (tr, ch2, tr) in 2-ch sp*, rep from * to * 2x and * to ** 1x, tr in same sp as first st, ch2, join with ss to 3rd ch of stch. Fasten off.
{22 sts on each side; 4 2-ch cnr sps}

CASPIAN

The world's largest inland body of water between Europe and Asia
Φ 41.934978, λ 50.668945

Using A, begin with mc.

R1: ch3 (stch), 15tr, join with ss to 3rd ch of stch. {16 sts}

R2: dc in same st as ss, *ch6, dc in next st, ch8**, dc in next st*, rep from * to * 6x and * to ** 1x, join with ss to first st. Fasten off. {16 sts, 8 6-ch sps, 8 8-ch sps}

R3: Attach B with ss to any 6-ch sp, ch3 (stch), 6tr in same sp, *skip (1 st, 8-ch sps and 1 st)**, 7tr in 6-ch sp*, rep from * to * 6x and * to ** 1x, join with ss to 3rd ch of stch. Fasten off. {56 sts}

R4: Attach C with stdg tr between any 7-st groups, *ch3, bpdc around 4th st of 7-st group, ch3**, tr between next 2 groups of 7 sts*, rep from * to * 6x and * to ** 1x, join with ss to first st. {16 sts, 16 3-ch sps}

R5: dc in same st as ss and 8-ch sp of R2 at the same time, *3dc in 3-ch sp, dc in next st, 3dc in 3-ch sp**, dc in 8-ch sp of R2 and next st at the same time*, rep from * to * 6x and * to ** 1x, join with ss to first st. {64 sts}

R6: ch4 (stch), dtr in same st as ss, *hdtr in next 2 sts, tr in next 11 sts, hdtr in next 2 sts**, 3dtr in next st*, rep from * to * 2x and * to ** 1x, dtr in same st as first sts, join with ss to 4th ch of stch. Fasten off. {15 sts on each side; 4 3-st cnrs}

R7: Attach D with stdg htr to middle st of any 3-st cnr, *8x [ch1, skip 1 st, htr in next st], ch1, skip 1 st**, (htr, ch3, htr) in next st*, rep from * to * 2x and * to ** 1x, htr in same st as first st, ch1, join with htr to first st. {10 sts, 9 1-ch sps on each side; 4 3-ch cnr sps}

R8: 2dc over joining htr, *9x [dc in next st, dc in 1-ch sp], dc in next st**, (2dc, ch2, 2dc) in 3-ch sp*, rep from * to * 2x and * to ** 1x, 2dc in same sp as first sts, ch2, join with ss to first st. Fasten off. {23 sts on each side; 4 2-ch cnr sps}

PERSIAN

A region of the northern Indian Ocean bounded on the north by Pakistan and Iran
Φ 26.750534, λ 51.683430

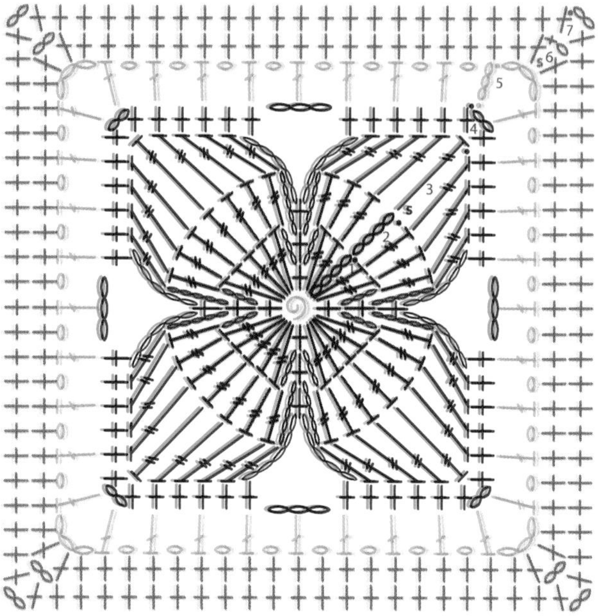

Using A, begin with mc.

R1: ch4 (stch), 2dtr, *ch3, dc, ch3**, 5dtr*, rep from * to * 2x and * to ** 1x, 2dtr, join with ss to 4th ch of stch. {24 sts, 8 3-ch sps}

R2: ch4 (stch), dtr in next 2 sts, *dtr in 3-ch sp, ch5, dc in next st, ch5, dtr in 3-ch sp**, dtr in next 5 sts*, rep from * to * 2x and * to ** 1x, dtr in next 2 sts, join with ss to 4th ch of stch. Fasten off. {32 sts, 8 5-ch sps}

R3: Attach B with stdg dtr to 4th st of a 7-st group, dtr in next 3 sts, *dtr in 5-ch sp, ch5, dc in next st, ch5, dtr in 5-ch sp**, dtr in next 7 sts*, rep from * to * 2x and * to ** 1x, dtr in next 3 sts, join with ss to first st. {40 sts, 8 5-ch sps}

R4: dc in same st as ss, *dc in next 4 sts, dc in 5-ch sp, ch3, skip 1 st, dc in 5-ch sp, dc in next 4 sts**, (dc, ch2, dc) in next st*, rep from * to * 2x and * to ** 1x, dc in same st as first st, ch2, join with ss to first st. Fasten off.
{12 sts, 1 3-ch sp on each side; 4 2-ch cnr sps}

R5: Attach C with ss to any 2-ch cnr sp, ch3 (stch), *3x [ch1, skip 1 st, tr in next st], ch1, tr in 3-ch sp, ch1, 3x [tr in next st, ch1, skip 1 st]**, (tr, ch3, tr) in 2-ch sp*, rep from * to * 2x and * to ** 1x, tr in same sp as first st, ch3, join with ss to 3rd ch of stch. Fasten off.
{9 sts, 8 1-ch sps on each side; 4 3-ch cnr sps}

R6: Attach D with stdg dc to any 3-ch cnr sp, dc in same sp, *8x [dc in next st, dc in 1-ch sp], dc in next st**, (2dc, ch2, 2dc) in 3-ch sp*, rep from * to * 2x and * to ** 1x, 2dc in same sp as first sts, ch1, join with dc to first st.
{21 sts on each side; 4 2-ch cnr sps}

R7: dc over joining dc, *dc in next 21 sts**, (dc, ch2, dc) in 2-ch sp*, rep from * to * 2x and * to ** 1x, dc in same sp as first st, ch2, join with ss to first st. Fasten off.
{23 sts on each side; 4 2-ch cnr sps}

ADEN

Connects with the Red Sea in the west and the Indian Ocean to the east
Φ 12.575943, λ 47.816970

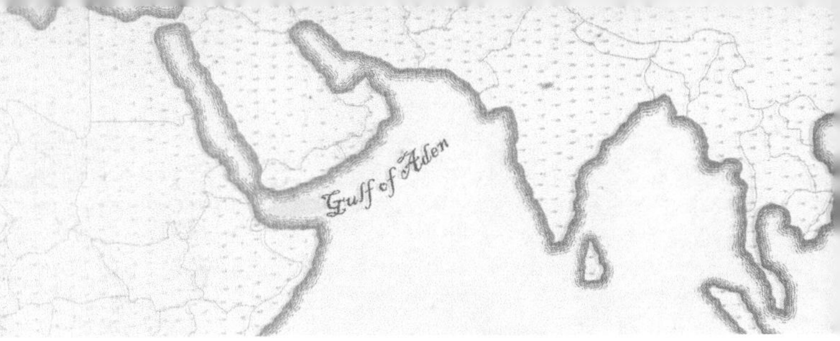

Using A, begin with mc.

R1: ch3 (stch), tr, *ch2, dtr, ch2**, 3tr*, rep from * to * 2x and * to ** 1x, tr, join with ss to 3rd ch of stch. {16 sts, 8 2-ch sps}

R2: dc in same st as ss, dc in next st, *(dc, htr) in 2-ch sp, (tr, hdtr, tr) in next st, (htr, dc) in 2-ch sp**, dc in next 3 sts*, rep from * to * 2x and * to ** 1x, dc in next st, join with ss to first st. Fasten off. {40 sts}

R3: Attach B with stdg tr to middle dc between points, *ch4, skip 4 sts, dc in next st, ch4, skip 4 sts**, (tr, ch2, tr) in next st*, rep from * to * 2x and * to ** 1x, tr in same st as first st, ch1, join with dc to first st.
{3 sts, 2 4-ch sps on each side; 4 2-ch cnr sps}

R4: ch3 (stch), 2tr over joining dc, *tr in next st, 3dc in 4-ch sp, dc in next st, 3dc in 4-ch sp, tr in next st**, 5tr in 2-ch sp*, rep from * to * 2x and * to ** 1x, 2tr in same sp as first sts, join with ss to 3rd ch of stch.
{9 sts on each side; 4 5-st cnrs}

R5: ch3 (stch), tr in same st as ss, *tr in next 13 sts**, (tr, hdtr, tr) in next st*, rep from * to * 2x and * to ** 1x, tr in same st as first sts, join with ss to 3rd ch of stch. Fasten off.
{13 sts on each side; 4 3-st cnrs}

R6: Attach C with stdg dc to middle st of any 3-st cnr, *7x [ch2, skip 1 st, dc in next st], ch2, skip 1 st**, (dc, ch2, dc) in next st*, rep from * to * 2x and * to ** 1x, dc in same st as first st, ch1, join with dc to first st.
{9 sts, 8 2-ch sps on each side; 4 2-ch cnr sps}

R7: dc over joining dc, *8x [dc in next st, dc in 2-ch sp], dc in next st**, (dc, ch2, dc) in 2-ch sp*, rep from * to * 2x and * to ** 1x, dc in same sp as first st, ch2, join with ss to first st. Fasten off.
{19 sts on each side; 4 2-ch cnr sps}

R8: Attach D with stdg dc to any 2-ch cnr sp, *dc in next 19 sts**, (dc, ch2, dc) in 2-ch sp*, rep from * to * 2x and * to ** 1x, dc in same sp as first st, ch1, join with dc to first st.
{21 sts on each side; 4 2-ch cnr sps}

R9: dc over joining dc, *dc in next 21 sts**, (dc, ch2, dc) in 2-ch sp*, rep from * to * 2x and * to ** 1x, dc in same sp as first st, ch2, join with ss to first st. Fasten off.
{23 sts on each side; 4 2-ch cnr sps}

MOZAMBIQUE

Located between the Southeast African countries of Madagascar and Mozambique
Φ -17.342249, λ 41.577957

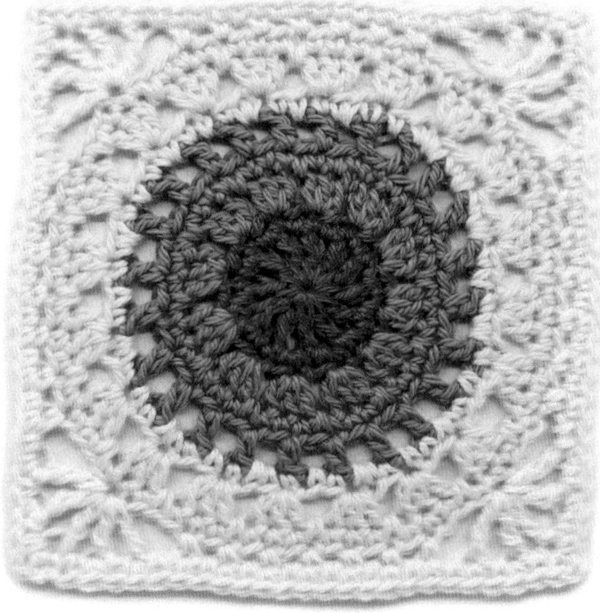

Using A, attach yarn to hook with a slip knot, ch1, work all R1 sts into that ch.

R1: ch3 (stch), *ch1, tr*, rep from * to * 10x, ch1, join with ss to 3rd ch of stch. {12 sts, 12 1-ch sps}

R2: dc in same st as ss, *dc in 1-ch sp**, dc in next st*, rep from * to * 10x and * to ** 1x, join with ss to first st. Fasten off. {24 sts}

R3: Attach B with stdg tr to any st, 2tr in same st, *skip 1 st**, 3tr in next st*, rep from * to * 10x and * to ** 1x, join with ss to first st. {36 sts}

R4: dc in same st as ss, dc in next 2 sts, *dc between last and next sts**, dc in next 3 sts*, rep from * to * 10x and * to ** 1x, join with ss to first st. {48 sts}

R5: ch3 (stch), *ch1, skip 1 st**, tr in next st*, rep from * to * 22x and * to ** 1x, join with ss to 3rd ch of stch. Fasten off. {24 sts, 24 1-ch sps}

R6: Attach C with stdg dc to any st, *2dc in 1-ch sp, dc in next st, dc in 1-ch sp**, dc in next st*, rep from * to * 10x and * to ** 1x, join with ss to first st. {60 sts}

R7: ch3 (stch), 2tr in same st as ss, *skip 2 sts**, 3tr in next st*, rep from * to * 18x and * to ** 1x, join with ss to 3rd ch of stch. {60 sts}

R8: dc in same st as ss, dc in next 2 sts, *dc between previous and next sts**, dc in next 3 sts*, rep from * to * 18x and * to ** 1x, join with ss to first st. Fasten off. {80 sts}

R9: Attach D with stdg dtr to any st, 2x [ch1, dtr] in same st, *ch1, skip 3 sts, 6x [dc in next st, ch1, skip 1 st], dc in next st, ch1, skip 3 sts**, (dtr, 4x [ch1, dtr]) in next st*, rep from * to * 2x and * to ** 1x, 2x [dtr, ch1] in same st as first sts, join with ss to first st.
{11 sts, 12 1-ch sps on each side; 4 1-st cnrs}

R10: dc in same st as ss, *11x [dc in 1-ch sp, dc in next st], dc in 1-ch sp**, (dc, ch2, dc) in next st*, rep from * to * 2x and * to ** 1x, dc in same st as first st, ch2, join with ss to first st. Fasten off. {25 sts on each side; 4 2-ch cnr sps}

BENGAL

Located in the Indian Ocean
Φ 13.205722, λ 89.162250

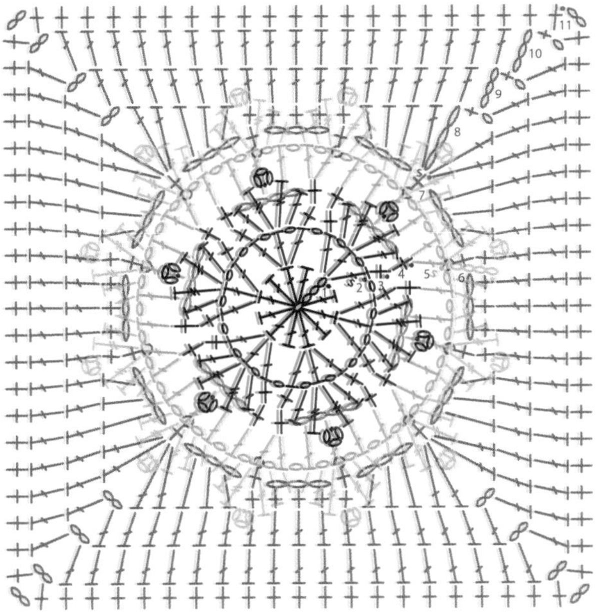

Using A, attach yarn to hook with a slip knot, ch1, work all R1 sts into that ch.

R1: ch3 (stch), 11tr, join with ss to 3rd ch of stch. Fasten off. {12 sts}

R2: Attach B with stdg tr to any st, 2x [ch1, tr] in same st as ss, *ch1, skip 1 st**, (2x [tr, ch1], tr) in next st*, rep from * to * 4x and * to ** 1x, join with ss to first st. {18 sts, 18 1-ch sps}

R3: dc in same st as ss, *tr in 1-ch sp, (dtr, picot, dtr) in next st, tr in 1-ch sp, dc in next st, skip 1-ch sp**, dc in next st*, rep from * to * 4x and * to ** 1x, join with ss to first st. {42 sts}

R4: dc in same st as ss, *ch4, skip 5 sts**, dc in next 2 sts*, rep from * to * 4x and * to ** 1x, dc in next st, join with ss to first st. Fasten off. {12 sts, 6 4-ch sps}

R5: Attach C with stdg tr to any dc before a 4-ch sp, ch1, tr in same st, *3x [ch1, tr] in 4-ch sp, ch1, tr in next st**, 2x [ch1, tr] in next st*, rep from * to * 4x and * to ** 1x, ch1, join with ss to first st. {36 sts, 36 1-ch sps}

R6: ch4 (stch), picot, dtr in same st as ss, *tr in 1-ch sp, dc in next st, skip 1-ch sp, dc in next st, tr in 1-ch sp**, (dtr, picot, dtr) in next st*, rep from * to * 10x and * to ** 1x, join with ss to 4th ch of stch. Fasten off. {84 sts}

R7: Attach D with stdg bpdc around the middle tr of any 3-tr group of R5, *ch3, skip 2 R5 sts**, bpdc around next R5 st*, rep from * to * 10x and * to ** 1x, join with ss to first st.
{12 sts, 12 3-ch sps}

R8: ch3 (stch), tr in same st as ss, *3htr in 3-ch sp, dc in next st, 3dc in 3-ch sp, dc in next st, 3htr in 3-ch sp**, (2tr, ch2, 2tr) in next st*, rep from * to * 2x and * to ** 1x, 2tr in same st as first sts, ch1, join with dc to 3rd ch of stch.
{15 sts on each side; 4 2-ch cnr sps}

R9: ch3 (stch), *tr in next 15 sts**, (tr, ch2, tr) in 2-ch sp*, rep from * to * 2x and * to ** 1x, tr in same sp as first st, ch1, join with dc to 3rd ch of stch. {17 sts on each side, 4 2-ch cnr sps}

R10: ch3 (stch), *tr in next 17 sts**, (tr, ch2, tr) in 2-ch sp*, rep from * to * 2x and * to ** 1x, tr in same sp as first st, ch1, join with dc to 3rd ch of stch. {19 sts on each side, 4 2-ch cnr sps}

R11: dc over joining dc, *dc in next 19 sts**, (dc, ch2, dc) in 2-ch sp*, rep from * to * 2x and * to ** 1x, dc in same sp as first st, ch2, join with ss to first st. Fasten off.
{21 sts on each side; 4 2-ch cnr sps}

ANDAMAN

A marginal sea of the eastern Indian Ocean
Φ 10.643333, λ 95.815325

Using A, begin with mc.

R1: ch3 (stch), *ch1, 5tr, ch1**, tr*, rep from * to * 4x and * to ** 1x, join with ss to 3rd ch of stch. {36 sts, 12 1-ch sps}

R2: ch3 (stch), *tr in 1-ch sp, tr in both 1-ch sps on either side of next 5 sts, tr in 1-ch sp**, 2tr in next st*, rep from * to * 4x and * to ** 1x, tr in same st as first st, join with ss to 3rd ch of stch. Fasten off. {30 sts}

R3: Attach B with stdg dc to 2nd tr of any 2tr in one st, dc in next st, *spike dc in 1-ch sp of R1, dc in next st, spike dc in 1-ch sp of R1**, dc in next 4 sts*, rep from * to * 4x and * to ** 1x, dc in next 2 sts, join with ss to first st. {42 sts}

R4: ch3 (stch), 2tr in same st as ss, *skip 2 sts, dc in next st, skip 2 sts, 3tr in next st**, ch2, 3tr in next st*, rep from * to * 4x and * to ** 1x, 3tr in next st, ch2, join with ss to 3rd ch of stch. Fasten off. {42 sts, 6 2-ch sps}

R5: Attach C with stdg dc to any 2-ch sp, *dc in blo of next st, htr in blo of next st, tr in blo of next st, ch1, 5tr in next st, ch1, tr in blo of next st, htr in blo of next st, dc in blo of next st**, dc in 2-ch sp*, rep from * to * 4x and * to ** 1x, join with ss to first st. {72 sts, 12 1-ch sps}

R6: dc in same st as ss, dc in next 3 sts, *dc in 1-ch sp, dc in both 1-ch sps on either side of the next 5 sts at the same time, dc in 1-ch sp*, dc in next 7 sts*, rep from * to * 4x and * to ** 1x, dc in next 3 sts, join with ss to first st. {60 sts}

R7: ch4 (stch), dtr in same st as ss, *skip 1 st, 3tr in next st, skip 2 sts, dc in next 6 sts, skip 2 sts, 3tr in next st, skip 1 st**, 3dtr in next st*, rep from * to * 2x and * to ** 1x, dtr in same st as first sts, join with ss to 4th ch of stch. Fasten off. {12 sts on each side; 4 3-st cnrs}

R8: Attach D with stdg dc to middle st of any 3-st cnr, *dc in next 14 sts**, (dc, ch2, dc) in next st*, rep from * to * 2x and * to ** 1x, dc in same st as first st, ch1, join with dc to first st. {16 sts on each side; 4 2-ch cnr sps}

R9: dc over joining dc, *dc in blo of next 16 sts**, (dc, ch2, dc) in 2-ch sp*, rep from * to * 2x and * to ** 1x, dc in same sp as first st, ch1, join with dc to first st. {18 sts on each side; 4 2-ch cnr sps}

R10: dc over joining dc, *dc in blo of next 18 sts**, (dc, ch2, dc) in 2-ch sp*, rep from * to * 2x and * to ** 1x, dc in same sp as first st, ch2, join with ss to first st. Fasten off. {20 sts on each side, 4 2-ch cnr sps}

BOHAI

The innermost gulf of the Yellow Sea
Φ 38.945739, λ 120.173406

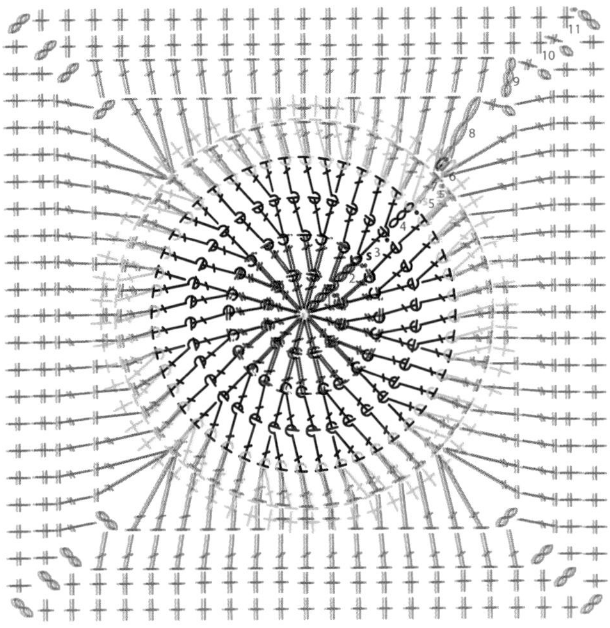

Using A, attach yarn to hook with a slip knot, ch1, work all R1 sts into the 1-ch sp.

R1: ch3 (stch), 11tr, join with ss to 3rd ch of stch. {12 sts}

R2: ch3 (stch), fptr around same st ss'd into, *tr in next st, fptr around same st*, rep from * to * 10x, join with ss to 3rd ch of stch. Fasten off. {24 sts}

R3: Attach B with stdg tr to any non-fp tr, fptr around same st, fptr around next st, *tr in next st, fptr around same st, fptr around next st*, rep from * to * 10x, join with ss to first st. {36 sts}

R4: ch3 (stch), fptr around same st ss'd into, fptr around next 2 sts, *tr in next st, fptr around same st, fptr around next 2 sts*, rep from * to * 10x, join with ss to 3rd ch of stch. Fasten off. {48 sts}

R5: Attach C with stdg tr to any non-fp tr, fptr around same st, fptr around next 3 sts, *tr in next st, fptr around same st, fptr around next 3 sts*, rep from * to * 10x, join with ss to first st. {60 sts}

R6: ch1, dc in next 59 sts, join with invisible join to first true st. Fasten off. {60 sts}

R7: Attach D with stdg tr to any st of R4, tr in next 47 sts of R4, join with ss to first st. {48 sts}
NOTE: work a st in every st of R4 even those worked into in R5.

R8: ch3 (stch), tr in same sp as ss, *tr in next st, htr in next 3 sts, dc in next 3 sts, htr in next 3 sts, tr in next st**, (2tr, ch2, 2tr) in next st*, rep from * to * 2x & * to ** 1x, 2tr in same sp as first sts, ch1, join with dc to 3rd ch of stch.
{15 sts on each side; 4 2-ch cnr sps}

R9: ch3 (stch), *tr in next 15 sts**, (tr, ch2, tr) in 2-ch sp*, rep from * to * 2x & * to ** 1x, tr in same sp as first st, ch1, join with dc to 3rd ch of stch. {17 sts on each side; 4 2-ch cnr sps}

R10: dc over joining dc, *dc in next 17 sts**, (dc, ch2, dc) in 2-ch sp*, rep from * to * 2x & * to ** 1x, dc in same sp as first st, ch1, join with dc to first st. {19 sts on each side; 4 2-ch cnr sps}

R11: dc over joining dc, *dc in next 19 sts**, (dc, ch2, dc) in 2-ch sp*, rep from * to * 2x & * to ** 1x, dc in same sp as first st, ch2, join with ss to first st. Fasten off.
{21 sts on each side; 4 2-ch cnr sps}

OKHOTSK

A marginal sea of the western Pacific Ocean
Φ 53.790268, λ 149.488306

Using A, attach yarn to hook with a slip knot, ch1, work all R1 sts into that ch.

R1: ch1, 8dc, join with ss to first st. {8 sts}

R2: 2dc in same st as ss, 2dc in next 7 sts, join with ss to first st. {16 sts}

R3: 2dc in same st as ss, *dc in next st**, 2dc in next st*, rep from * to * 6x and * to ** 1x, join with ss to first st. {24 sts}

R4: dc in same st as ss, dc in next st, 2dc in next st, *dc in next 2 sts, 2dc in next st*, rep from * to * 6x, join with ss to first st. Fasten off. {32 sts}

R5: Attach B with stdg tr to any st, *skip 1 st**, (tr, ch1, tr) in next st*, rep from * to * 14x and * to ** 1x, tr in same st as first st, join with dc to first st. {32 sts, 16 1-ch sps}

R6: dc over joining dc, *skip 1 st, spike dc in skipped st of R4 below, skip 1 st**, dc in 1-ch sp*, rep from * to * 14x and * to ** 1x, join with ss to first st. Fasten off. {32 sts}

R7: Attach C with ss to any 1-ch sp of R5 and over dc of R6, ch3 (stch), 4tr in same sp, *ch1, puff in next st**, ch1, 5tr in 1-ch sp of R5 and over dc of R6*, rep from * to * 14x and * to ** 1x, join with dc to 3rd ch of stch. {96 sts, 32 1-ch sps}

R8: dc over joining dc and in 1-ch sp after the next 5 sts at the same time, *dc in 1-ch sp, dc in next st, dc in 1-ch sp**, dc in both 1-ch sps on either side of the next 5 sts at the same time*, rep from * to * 14x and * to ** 1x, join with ss to first st. Fasten off. {64 sts}

R9: Attach D with stdg dc to any st, dc in next 63 sts, join with ss to first st. {64 sts}

R10: dc in same st as ss, dc in next 63 sts, join with ss to first st. {64 sts}

R11: ch3 (stch), 3tr in same st as ss, *skip 2 sts, dc in next 11 sts, skip 2 sts**, 7tr in next st*, rep from * to * 2x and * to ** 1x, 3tr in same st as first sts, join with ss to 3rd ch of stch.
{11 sts on each side; 4 7-st cnrs}

R12: dc in same st as ss, *dc in next 2 sts, htr in next 2 sts, dc in next 9 sts, htr in next 2 sts, dc in next 2 sts**, (dc, ch2, dc) in next st*, rep from * to * 2x and * to ** 1x, dc in same st as first st, ch1, join with dc to first st.
{19 sts on each side; 4 2-ch cnr sps}

R13: dc over joining dc, *dc in next 19 sts**, (dc, ch2, dc) in 2-ch sp*, rep from * to * 2x and * to ** 1x, dc in same sp as first st, ch2, join with ss to first st. Fasten off.
{21 sts on each side; 4 2-ch cnr sps}

SETO

Connecting the Pacific Ocean to the Sea of Japan
Φ 34.118171, λ 133.382740

Using A, attach yarn to hook with a slip knot, ch1, work all R1 sts into that ch.

R1: ch3 (stch), 11tr, join with ss to 3rd ch of stch. {12 sts}

R2: ch3 (stch), tr in same st as ss, *skip 1 st, 3tr in next st*, rep from * to * 4x, skip 1 st, tr in same st as first sts, join with ss to 3rd ch of stch. {18 sts}

R3: ch3 (stch), 4tr in same st as ss, *skip 1 st, dc between last and next st, skip 1 st**, 5tr in next st*, rep from * to * 4x and * to ** 1x, join with ss to 3rd ch of stch. Fasten off. {36 sts}

R4: Attach B with stdg spike dc to any middle st of a 3-st group of R2, *ch5, skip 5 sts**, spike dc in middle st of next 3-st group of R2*, rep from * to * 4x and * to ** 1x, join with ss to first st. {6 sts, 6 5-ch sps}

R5: ch3 (stch), *6tr in 5-ch sp**, tr in next st*, rep from * to * 4x and * to ** 1x, join with ss to 3rd ch of stch. {42 sts}

R6: ch3 {stch}, *spike tr into spike st of R4**, tr in next 7 sts*, rep from * to * 4x and * to ** 1x, tr in next 6 sts, join with ss to 3rd ch of stch. Fasten off. {48 sts}

R7: Attach C with stdg tr to blo of any st, tr in same blo, *tr in blo of next st, htr in blo of next 3 sts, dc in blo of next 3 sts, htr in blo of next 3 sts, tr in blo of next st**, (2tr, ch2, 2tr) in blo of next st*, rep from * to * 2x and * to ** 1x, 2tr in same blo as first sts, ch1, join with dc to first st. {15 sts on each side; 4 2-ch cnr sps}

R8: ch3 (stch), *tr in next 15 sts**, (tr, ch2, tr) in 2-ch sp*, rep from * to * 2x and * to ** 1x, tr in same sp as first st, ch2, join with ss to 3rd ch of stch. Fasten off. {17 sts on each side; 4 2-ch cnr sps}

R9: Attach D with stdg dc to any 2-ch cnr sp, *bpdc around next 17 sts**, (dc, ch2, dc) in 2-ch sp*, rep from * to * 2x and * to ** 1x, dc in same sp as first st, ch1, join with dc to first st. {19 sts on each side; 4 2-ch cnr sps}

R10: dc over joining dc, *dc in next 19 sts**, (dc, ch2, dc) in 2-ch sp*, rep from * to * 2x and * to ** 1x, dc in same sp as first st, ch2, join with ss to first st. Fasten off. {21 sts on each side; 4 2-ch cnr sps}

VISAYAN

Located in the Philippines
Φ 11.557800, λ 123.852200

Using A, begin with mc.

R1: ch3 (stch), 19tr, join with ss to 3rd ch of stch. {20 sts}

R2: ch1 (stch), dc in next 19 sts, join with inv join to first true dc. Fasten off. {20 sts}

R3: Attach B with stdg tr to blo of any st, *ch1**, tr in blo of next st*, rep from * to * 18x and * to ** 1x, join with ss to first st. {20 sts, 20 1-ch sps}

R4: ch1 (stch), *dc in 1-ch sp**, dc in next st*, rep from * to * 18x and * to ** 1x, join with inv join to first true dc. Fasten off. {40 sts}

R5: Attach C with stdg tr to blo of any st, *ch1**, tr in blo of next st*, rep from * to * 38x and * to ** 1x, join with ss to first st. {40 sts, 40 1-ch sps}

R6: ch1 (stch), dc in 1-ch sp, dc in next st, dc2tog over 1-ch sp and next st, *dc in 1-ch sp, dc in next st, dc in 1-ch sp, dc2tog over next st and 1-ch sp**, dc in next st, dc in 1-ch sp, dc in next st, dc2tog over 1-ch sp and next st*, rep from * to * 6x and * to ** 1x, join with inv join to first true dc. Fasten off. {64 sts}

R7: Attach D with stdg dtr to blo of any st, hdtr in same blo, *tr in blo of next 3 sts, htr in blo of next 3 sts, dc in blo of next 3 sts, htr in blo of next 3 sts, tr in blo of next 3 sts**, (hdtr, dtr, ch2, dtr, hdtr) in blo of next st*, rep from * to * 2x and * to ** 1x, (hdtr, dtr) in same blo as first sts, ch1, join with dc to first st.
{19 sts on each side; 4 2-ch cnr sps}

R8: dc over joining dc, *dc in next 19 sts**, (dc, ch2, dc) in 2-ch sp*, rep from * to * 2x and * to ** 1x, dc in same sp as first st, ch1, join with dc to first st. {21 sts on each side; 4 2-ch cnr sps}

R9: dc over joining dc, *dc in next 21 sts**, (dc, ch2, dc) in 2-ch sp*, rep from * to * 2x and * to ** 1x, dc in same sp as first st, ch2, join with ss to first st. Fasten off.
{23 sts on each side; 4 2-ch cnr sps}

SIBUYAN

Located in the Philippines
Φ 12.666667, λ 122.500000

Using A, begin with mc.

R1: ch3 (stch), tr around stch, *tr, tr around tr just made*, rep from * to * 6x, join with ss to 3rd ch of stch. {16 sts}

R2: ch3 (stch), tr around stch, *tr in next st, tr around tr just made*, rep from * to * 14x, join with ss to 3rd ch of stch. {32 sts}

R3: dc in same st as ss, dc in next 31 sts, join with ss to first st. Fasten off. {32 sts}

R4: Attach B with stdg spike dc between sts of R2, *ch2, skip 1 st**, spike dc between sts of R2*, rep from * to * 14x & * to ** 1x, join with ss to first st. {16 sts, 16 2-ch sps}

R5: ch3 (stch), *ch1, puff in 2-ch sp, ch1**, tr in next st*, rep from * to * 14x and * to ** 1x, join with ss to 3rd ch of stch. Fasten off.
{32 sts, 32 1-ch sps}

R6: Attach C with stdg dc to any tr, *ch3, skip (1-ch sp, 1 st and 1-ch sp)**, dc in next st*, rep from * to * 14x and * to ** 1x, join with ss to first st.
{16 sts, 16 3-ch sps}

R7: dc in same st as ss, *3dc in 3-ch sp**, dc in next st*, rep from * to * 14x and * to ** 1x, join with ss to first st. {64 sts}

R8: ch3 (stch), tr in same st as ss, *tr in next 2 sts, htr in next 3 sts, dc in next 5 sts, htr in next 3 sts, tr in next 2 sts**, (tr, hdtr, tr) in next st*, rep from * to * 2x and * to ** 1x, tr in same st as first sts, join with ss to 3rd ch of stch. Fasten off. {17 sts on each side; 4 1-st cnr sps}

R9: Attach D with stdg dc to any hdtr, *dc in next 17 sts**, (dc, ch2, dc) in next st*, rep from * to * 2x and * to ** 1x, dc in same st as first st, ch1, join with dc to first st.
{19 sts on each side; 4 2-ch cnr sps}

R10: ch2 (stch), *htr in next 19 sts**, (htr, ch2, htr) in 2-ch sp*, rep from * to * 2x and * to ** 1x, htr in same sp as first st, ch2, join with ss to 2nd ch of stch. Fasten off.
{21 sts on each side; 4 2-ch cnr sps}

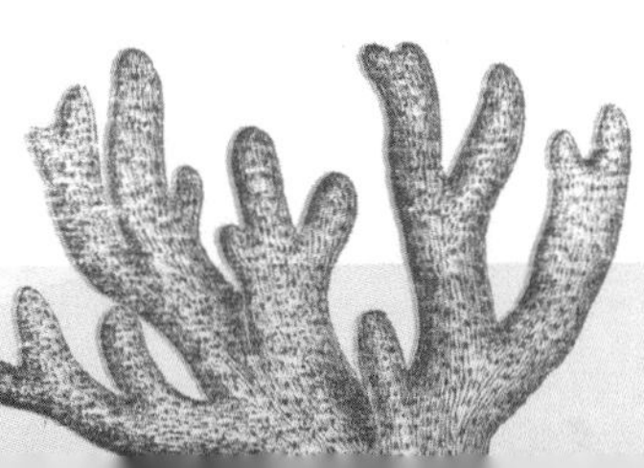

SULU

A sea in the southwestern area of the Philippines
Φ 3.478325, λ 123.210650

Using A, begin with mc.

R1: ch3 (stch), 15tr, join with ss to 3rd ch of stch. {16 sts}

R2: ch3 (stch), tr in same st as ss, *fptr around next st, tr in next st, fptr around next st**, 3tr in next st*, rep from * to * 2x and * to ** 1x, tr in same st as first sts, join with ss to 3rd ch of stch. {3 sts on each side; 4 3-st cnrs}

R3: ch3 (stch), tr in same st as ss, *skip 1 st, fptr around next st, tr in st just worked around, bptr around next st, tr in next st, fptr around st just worked into, skip 1 st**, 3tr in next st*, rep from * to * 2x and * to ** 1x, tr in same st as first sts, join with ss to 3rd ch of stch. Fasten off. {5 sts on each side; 4 3-st cnrs}

R4: Attach B with stdg tr to middle st of any 3-st cnr, tr in same st, *tr in next st, fptr around next st, tr in st just worked around, bptr around next 3 sts, tr in next st, fptr around st just worked into, tr in next st**, 3tr in next st*, rep from * to * 2x and * to ** 1x, tr in same st as first sts, join with ss to first st. {9 sts on each side; 4 3-st cnrs}

R5: ch3 (stch), tr in same st as ss, *tr in next 2 sts, fptr around next st, tr in st just worked around, bptr around next 5 sts, tr in next st, fptr around st just worked into, tr in next 2 sts**, 3tr in next st*, rep from * to * 2x and * to ** 1x, tr in same st as first sts, join with ss to 3rd ch of stch. Fasten off. {13 sts on each side; 4 3-st cnrs}

R6: Attach C with stdg tr to middle st of any 3-st cnr, tr in same st, *tr in next 3 sts, fptr around next st, tr in st just worked around, bptr around next 7 sts, tr in next st, fptr around st just worked into, tr in next 3 sts**, 3tr in next st*, rep from * to * 2x and * to ** 1x, tr in same st as first sts, join with ss to first st. {17 sts on each side; 4 3-st cnrs}

R7: ch3 (stch), tr in same st as ss, *tr in next 3 sts, skip 1 st, fptr around next st, tr in st just worked around, bptr around next 9 sts, tr in next st, fptr around st just worked into, skip 1 st, tr in next 3 sts**, 3tr in next st*, rep from * to * 2x and * to ** 1x, tr in same st as first sts, join with ss to 3rd ch of stch. Fasten off. {19 sts on each side; 4 3-st cnrs}

R8: Attach D with stdg dc to middle st of any 3-st cnr, *dc in next 21 sts**, (dc, ch2, dc) in next st*, rep from * to * 2x and * to ** 1x, dc in same st as first st, ch2, join with ss to first st. Fasten off. {23 sts on each side; 4 2-ch cnr sps}

JAVA

Located between the Indonesian islands
Φ -5.090944, λ 112.170410

Using A, attach yarn to hook with a slip knot, ch1, work all R1 sts into that ch.

R1: ch3 (stch), 2tr, *ch2, 3tr*, rep from * to * 2x, ch1, join with dc to 3rd ch of stch.
{3 sts on each side; 4 2-ch cnr sps}

R2: ch3 (stch), *ch1, skip 1 st, (tr, ch2, tr) in next st, ch1, skip 1 st**, (tr, ch2, tr) in 2-ch sp*, rep from * to * 2x and * to ** 1x, tr in same sp as first st, ch2, join with ss to 3rd ch of stch. Fasten off.
{4 sts, 2 1-ch sps, 1 2-ch sp on each side; 4 2-ch cnr sps}

R3: Attach B with stdg tr to any 2-ch cnr sp, *ch1, skip 1 st, tr in 1-ch sp, ch1, skip 1 st, 5tr in 2-ch sp, ch1, skip 1 st, tr in 1-ch sp, ch1, skip 1 st**, (tr, ch2, tr) in 2-ch sp*, rep from * to * 2x and * to ** 1x, tr in same sp as first st, ch1, join with dc to first st.
{9 sts, 4 1-ch sps on each side; 4 2-ch cnr sps}

R4: ch3 (stch), *2x [ch1, skip 1 st, tr in 1-ch sp], tr in next 2 sts, 2tr in next st, tr in next 2 sts, 2x [tr in 1-ch sp, ch1, skip 1 st]**, (tr, ch2, tr) in 2-ch sp*, rep from * to * 2x and * to ** 1x, tr in same sp as first st, ch2, join with ss to 3rd ch of stch. Fasten off.
{12 sts, 4 1-ch sps on each side; 4 2-ch cnr sps}

R5: Attach C with stdg tr to any 2-ch cnr sp, *2x [ch1, skip 1 st, tr in 1-ch sp], tr in next 8 sts, 2x [tr in 1-ch sp, ch1, skip 1 st]**, (tr, ch2, tr) in 2-ch sp*, rep from * to * 2x and * to ** 1x, tr in same sp as first st, ch1, join with dc to first st.
{14 sts, 4 1-ch sps on each side; 4 2-ch cnr sps}

R6: ch3 (stch), *2x [ch1, skip 1 st, tr in 1-ch sp], tr in next st, htr in next st, dc in next 6 sts, htr in next st, tr in next st, 2x [tr in 1-ch sp, ch1, skip 1 st]**, (tr, ch2, tr) in 2-ch sp*, rep from * to * 2x and * to ** 1x, tr in same sp as first st, ch2, join with ss to 3rd ch of stch. Fasten off.
{16 sts, 4 1-ch sps on each side; 4 2-ch cnr sps}

R7: Attach D with stdg dc to any 2-ch cnr sp, *2x [dc in next st, dc in 1-ch sp], dc in next 12 sts, 2x [dc in 1-ch sp, dc in next st]**, (dc, ch2, dc) in 2-ch sp*, rep from * to * 2x and * to ** 1x, dc in same sp as first st, ch2, join with ss to first st. Fasten off. {22 sts on each side; 4 2-ch cnr sps}

CELEBES

Located in the western Pacific Ocean
Φ 3.460785, λ 122.304729

☆ *bp sts are worked from the back each time. ch sps are behind the previous round up to and including R7.*

Using A, attach yarn to hook with a slip knot, ch1, work all R1 sts into that ch.

R1: ch1, *dc, ch2*, rep from * to * 6x, dc, ch1, join with dc to first st. {8 sts, 8 2-ch sps}

R2: dc over joining dc, *ch3, skip (1 st, 2-ch sp and 1 st)**, (dc, ch2, dc) in 2-ch sp*, rep from * to * 2x and * to ** 1x, dc in same sp as first st, ch1, join with dc to first st.
{2 sts, 1 3-ch sp on each side; 4 2-ch cnr sps}

R3: ch3 (stch), 2tr over joining dc, *ch1, skip (1 st and 3-ch sp), ss in 2-ch sp of R1 below in front of 3-ch sp, ch1, skip 1 st**, 5tr in 2-ch sp*, rep from * to * 2x and * to ** 1x, 2tr in same sp as first sts, join with ss to 3rd ch of stch. Fasten off. {1 st, 2 1-ch sps on each side; 4 5-st cnrs}

R4: Attach B with stdg dc to middle st of any 5-st cnr, *skip (2 sts and 1-ch sp), 7tr in 3-ch sp of R2 behind R3, skip (1-ch sp and 2 sts)**, (dc, ch2, dc) in next st*, rep from * to * 2x and * to ** 1x, dc in same st as first st, ch1, join with dc to first st. {9 sts on each side; 4 2-ch cnr sps}

R5: ch3 (stch), 2tr over joining dc, *ch1, skip 1 st, dc in next st, ch3, bpdc around ss of R3 below, ch3, skip 5 sts, dc in next st, ch1, skip 1 st**, 5tr in 2-ch sp*, rep from * to * 2x and * to ** 1x, 2tr in same st as first sts, join with ss to 3rd ch of stch. Fasten off.
{3 sts, 2 1-ch sps, 2 3-ch sps on each side; 4 5-st cnrs}

R6: Attach C with stdg dc to middle st of any 5-st cnr, *ch1, skip (2 sts, 1-ch sp and 1 st), 3htr in 3-ch sp, 5tr in next st, 3htr in 3-ch sp, ch1, skip (1 st, 1-ch sp and 2 sts)**, (dc, ch2, dc) in next st*, rep from * to * 2x and * to ** 1x, dc in same st as first st, ch1, join with dc to first st.
{13 sts, 2 1-ch sps on each side; 4 2-ch cnr sps}

R7: ch3 (stch), 2tr over joining dc, *ch1, skip (1 st and 1-ch sp), dc in next st, ch4, bpdc around bpdc of R5 below, ch4, skip 9 sts, dc in next st, ch1, skip (1-ch sp and 1 st)**, 5tr in 2-ch sp*, rep from * to * 2x and * to ** 1x, 2tr in same sp as first sts, join with ss to 3rd ch of stch. Fasten off.
{3 sts, 2 1-ch sps, 2 4-ch sps on each side; 4 5-st cnrs}

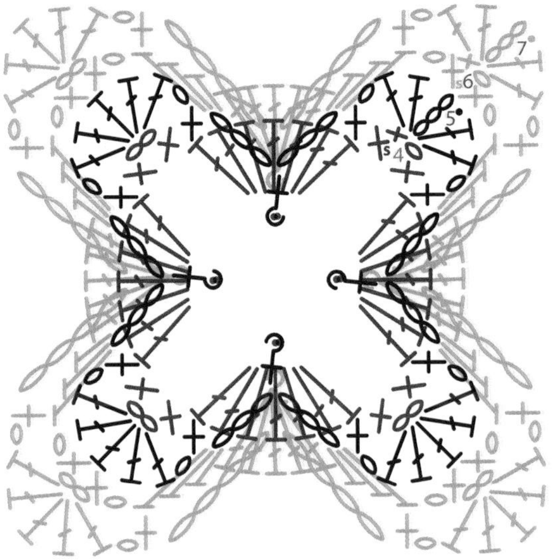

R8: Attach D with stdg dc to middle st of any 5-st cnr, *ch1, skip (2 sts, 1-ch sp and 1 st), 4 htr in 4-ch sp, 7tr in next st, 4 htr in 4-ch sp, ch1, skip (1 st, 1-ch sp and 2 sts)**, (dc, ch2, dc) in next st*, rep from * to * 2x and * to ** 1x, dc in same st as first st, ch1, join with dc to first st.
{17 sts on each side; 4 2-ch cnr sps}

R9: ch3 (stch), 2tr over joining dc, *ch1, skip (1 st and 1-ch sp), dc in next st, ch2, skip 3 sts, htr in lbv of next 2 sts, dc in lbv of next 3 sts, htr in lbv of next 2 sts, ch2, skip 3 sts, dc in next st, ch1, skip (1-ch sp and 1 st)**, 5tr in 2-ch sp*, rep from * to * 2x and * to ** 1x, 2tr in same sp as first sts, join with ss to 3rd ch of stch.
{9 sts, 2 1-ch sps, 2 2-ch sps on each side; 4 5-st cnrs}

R10: dc in same st as ss, *dc in next 2 sts, dc in 1-ch sp, dc in next st, 2dc in 2-ch sp, dc in next 7 sts, 2dc in 2-ch sp, dc in next st, dc in 1-ch sp, dc in next 2 sts**, (dc, ch2, dc) in next st*, rep from * to * 2x and * to ** 1x, dc in same st as first st, ch1, join with dc to first st.
{21 sts on each side; 4 2-ch cnr sps}

R11: dc over joining dc, *dc in next 21 sts**, (dc, ch2, dc) in 2-ch sp*, rep from * to * 2x and * to ** 1x, dc in same sp as first st, ch1, join with dc to first st. {23 sts on each side; 4 2-ch cnr sps}

R12: dc over joining dc, *dc in next 23 sts**, (dc, ch2, dc) in 2-ch sp*, rep from * to * 2x and * to ** 1x, dc in same sp as first st, ch2, join with ss to first st. Fasten off.
{25 sts on each side; 4 2-ch cnr sps}

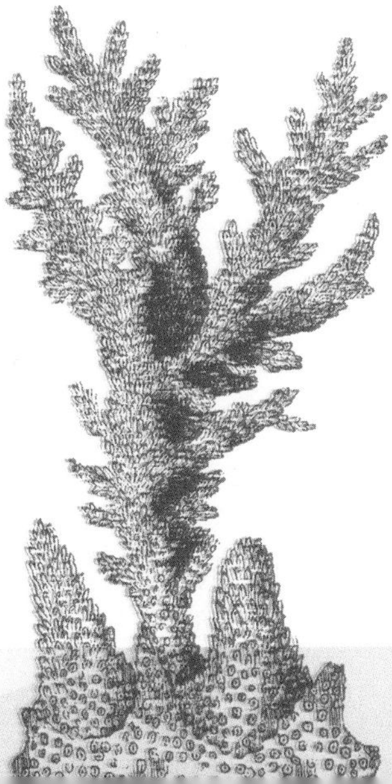

MOLUCCA

Located in the western Pacific Ocean
Φ -0.483392, λ 124.872603

Using A, begin with mc.

R1: ch3 (stch), tr, *ch2**, 3tr*, rep from * to * 4x and * to ** 1x, tr, join with ss to 3rd ch of stch. {18 sts, 6 2-ch sps}

R2: ch3 (stch), 4tr in same st as ss, *ch4, skip (1 st, 2-ch sp and 1 st), 5tr in next st*, rep from * to * 4x, ch3, join with dc to 3rd ch of stch. {30 sts, 6 4-ch sps}

R3: dc over joining dc and in 4-ch sp on the other side of the next 5 sts at the same time, *ch2, tr in 2-ch sp of R1 over 4-ch sp of R2, ch2**, dc in both 4-ch sps on either side of the next 5 sts at the same time*, rep from * to * 4x and * to ** 1x, join with ss to first st. Fasten off. {12 sts, 12 2-ch sps}

R4: Attach B with ss to any dc, ch3 (stch), *2tr in 2-ch sp, ch1, 5tr in next st, ch1, 2tr in 2-ch sp**, tr in next st*, rep from * to * 4x and * to ** 1x, join with ss to 3rd ch of stch. Fasten off. {60 sts, 12 1-ch sps}

R5: Attach C with stdg tr to any tr in a st on its own, *tr2tog over next 2 sts, ch2, tr in both 1-ch sps on either side of next 5 sts at the same time, ch2, tr2tog over next 2 sts**, tr in next st*, rep from * to * 4x and * to ** 1x, join with ss to first st. {24 sts, 12 2-ch sps}

R6: dc in same st as ss, dc in next st, *2dc in 2-ch sp, 2dc in next st, 2dc in 2-ch sp**, dc in next 3 sts*, rep from * to * 4x and * to ** 1x, dc in next st, join with ss to first st. {54 sts}

R7: ch3 (stch), tr in next st, *fphdtr around tr2tog of R5 below, tr in next 3 sts, fphdtr around next st of R5 below, tr in next 3 sts, fphdtr around tr2tog of R5 below**, tr in next 3 sts*, rep from * to * 4x and * to ** 1x, tr in next st, join with ss to 3rd ch of stch. Fasten off. {72 sts}

R8: Attach D with stdg dtr to any st between 2 tr2tog, hdtr in same st, *tr in next 2 sts, htr in next 3 sts, dc in next 7 sts, htr in next 3 sts, tr in next 2 sts**, (hdtr, dtr, ch2, dtr, hdtr) in next st*, rep from * to * 2x and * to ** 1x, (hdtr, dtr) in same st as first sts, ch1, join with dc to first st. {21 sts on each side; 4 2-ch cnr sps}

R9: dc over joining dc, *10x [dc in blo of next st, dc in next st], dc in blo of next st**, (dc, ch2, dc) in 2-ch sp*, rep from * to * 2x and * to ** 1x, dc in same sp as first st, ch2, join with ss to first st. Fasten off. {23 sts on each side; 4 2-ch cnr sps}

Flores

Located in Indonesia
Φ -7.702282, λ 119.675238

Using A, ch8, join last ch to first with a ss over the top 2 strands of the first ch.

R1: ch3 (stch), tr in same ch as ss, 2tr in next 7 chs, join with ss to 3rd ch of stch. Fasten off. {16 sts}

R2: Attach B with stdg dc to any st, *ch6, dc in next st* rep from * to * 14x, ch6, join with ss to first st. Fasten off. {16 sts, 16 6-ch sps}

R3: Attach C with stdg dc to any st, *ch2, push 6-ch sp forward, dc in next st*, rep from * to * 14x, ch2, join with ss to first st. {16 sts, 16 2-ch sps}

R4: ch3 (stch), *skip 2-ch sp, 2x [dc in next st, 2dc in 2-ch sp], dc in next st, skip 2-ch sp**, (tr, ch4, tr) in next st*, rep from * to * 2x and * to ** 1x, tr in same st as first st, ch1, join with tr to 3rd ch of stch. {9 sts on each side; 4 4-ch cnr sps}

R5: ch3 (stch), 4tr over joining tr, *skip 2 sts, dc in next 5 sts, skip 2 sts**, 9tr in 4-ch sp*, rep from * to * 2x and * to ** 1x, 4tr in same sp as first sts, join with ss to 3rd ch of stch.
{5 sts on each side; 4 9-st cnrs}

R6: ch3 (stch), tr in same st as ss, *2tr in next 3 sts, tr in next st, skip 2 sts, dc in next st, skip 2 sts, tr in next st, 2tr in next 3 sts**, 3tr in next st*, rep from * to * 2x and * to ** 1x, tr in same st as first sts, join with ss to 3rd ch of stch. Fasten off.
{15 sts on each side; 4 3-st cnrs}

R7: Attach D with stdg dc to middle st of any 3-st cnr, *dc in blo of next 5 sts, htr in blo of next 3 sts, tr in blo of next st, htr in blo of next 3 sts, dc in blo of next 5 sts**, (dc, ch2, dc) in next st*, rep from * to * 2x and * to ** 1x, dc in same st as first st, ch1, join with dc to first st.
{19 sts on each side; 4 2-ch cnr sps}

R8: dc over joining dc, *dc in next 19 sts**, (dc, ch2, dc) in 2-ch sp*, rep from * to * 2x and * to ** 1x, dc in same sp as first st, ch1, join with dc to first st. {21 sts on each side; 4 2-ch cnr sps}

R9: dc over joining dc, *dc in next 21 sts**, (dc, ch2, dc) in 2-ch sp*, rep from * to * 2x and * to ** 1x, dc in same sp as first st, ch2, join with ss to first st. Fasten off.
{23 sts on each side; 4 2-ch cnr sps}

BANDA

Located in the Maluku Islands of Indonesia
Φ -5.895817, λ 127.203109

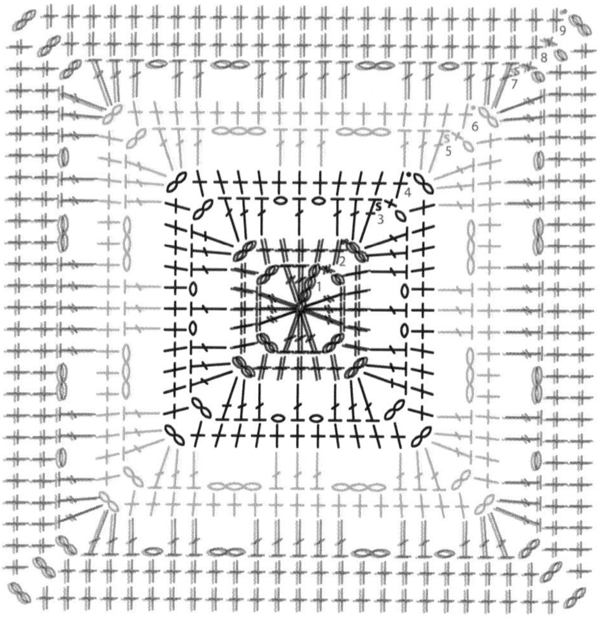

Using A, attach yarn to hook with a slip knot, ch1, work all R1 sts into that ch.

R1: ch3 (stch), 2tr, *ch2, 3tr*, rep from * to * 2x, ch1, join with dc to 3rd ch of stch.
{3 sts on each side; 4 2-ch cnr sps}

R2: dc over joining dc, *dc in next 3 sts**, (dc, ch2, dc) in 2-ch sp*, rep from * to * 2x and * to ** 1x, dc in same sp as first st, ch2, join with ss to first st. Fasten off.
{5 sts on each side; 4 2-ch cnr sps}

R3: Attach B with stdg tr to any 2-ch cnr sp, tr in same sp, *2x [tr in next st, ch1, skip 1 st], tr in next st**, (2tr, ch2, 2tr) in 2-ch sp*, rep from * to * 2x and * to ** 1x, 2tr in same sp as first sts, ch1, join with dc to first st.
{7 sts, 2 1-ch sps on each side; 4 2-ch cnr sps}

R4: dc over joining dc, *dc in next 3 sts, dc in 1-ch sp, dc in next st, dc in 1-ch sp, dc in next 3 sts**, (dc, ch2, dc) in 2-ch sp*, rep from * to * 2x and * to ** 1x, dc in same sp as first st, ch2, join with ss to first st. Fasten off.
{11 sts on each side; 4 2-ch cnr sps}

R5: Attach C with stdg tr to any 2-ch cnr sp, tr in same sp, *tr in next st, ch3, skip 3 sts, tr in next 3 sts, ch3, skip 3 sts, tr in next st**, (2tr, ch2, 2tr) in 2-ch sp*, rep from * to * 2x and * to ** 1x, 2tr in same sp as first sts, ch1, join with dc to first st.
{9 sts, 2 3-ch sps on each side; 4 2-ch cnr sps}

R6: dc over joining dc, *2x [dc in next 3 sts, 3dc in 3-ch sp], dc in next 3 sts**, (dc, ch2, dc) in 2-ch sp*, rep from * to * 2x and * to ** 1x, dc in same sp as first st, ch2, join with ss to first st. Fasten off. {17 sts on each side; 4 2-ch cnr sps}

R7: Attach D with stdg tr to any 2-ch cnr sp, tr in same sp, *tr in next st, ch1, skip 1 st, tr in next 2 sts, ch2, skip 2 sts, tr in next 5 sts, ch2, skip 2 sts, tr in next 2 sts, ch1, skip 1 st, tr in next st**, (2tr, ch2, 2tr) in 2-ch sp*, rep from * to * 2x and * to ** 1x, 2tr in same sp as first sts, ch1, join with dc to first st.
{15 sts, 2 1-ch sps, 2 2-ch sps on each side; 4 2-ch cnr sps}

R8: dc over joining dc, *dc in next 3 sts, dc in 1-ch sp, dc in next 2 sts, 2dc in 2-ch sp, dc in next 5 sts, 2dc in 2-ch sp, dc in next 2 sts, dc in 1-ch sp, dc in next 3 sts**, (dc, ch2, dc) in 2-ch sp*, rep from * to * 2x and * to ** 1x, dc in same sp as first st, ch1, join with dc to first st.
{23 sts on each side; 4 2-ch cnr sps}

R9: dc over joining dc, *dc in next 23 sts**, (dc, ch2, dc) in 2-ch sp*, rep from * to * 2x and * to ** 1x, dc in same sp as first st, ch2, join with ss to first st. Fasten off.
{25 sts on each side; 4 2-ch cnr sps}

CERAM

Located between the islands of Indonesia
Φ -2.697247, λ 130.747180

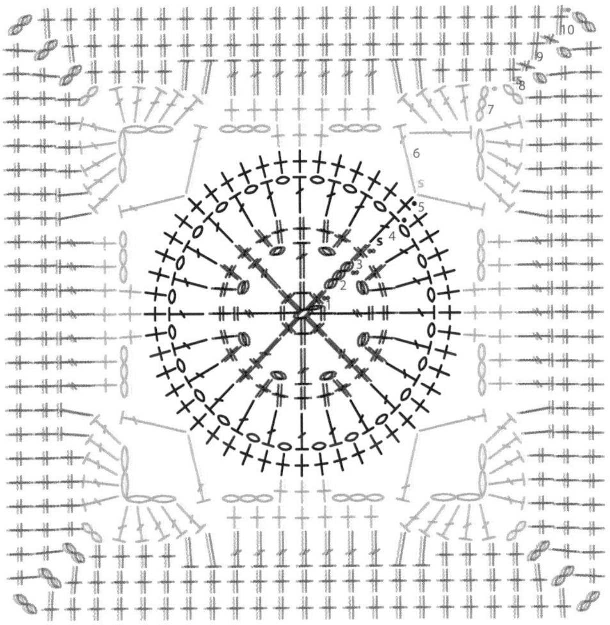

Using A, attach yarn to hook with a slip knot, ch1, work all R1 sts into that ch.

R1: ch1, 8dc, join with ss to first st. {8 sts}

R2: ch3 (stch), *ch1**, tr in next st*, rep from * to * 6x and * to ** 1x, join with ss to 3rd ch of stch. {8 sts, 8 1-ch sps}

R3: dc in same st as ss, *2dc in 1-ch sp**, dc in next st*, rep from * to * 6x and * to ** 1x, join with ss to first st. Fasten off. {24 sts}

R4: Attach B with stdg tr to any st in a st, *ch1**, tr in next st*, rep from * to * 22x and * to ** 1x, join with ss to first st. {24 sts, 24 1-ch sps}

R5: dc in same st as ss, *dc in 1-ch sp**, dc in next st*, rep from * to * 22x and * to ** 1x, join with ss to first st. Fasten off. {48 sts}

R6: Attach C with stdg tr to any st in a st, *ch3, skip 4 sts, dc in next 3 sts, ch3, skip 4 sts**, (tr, ch4, tr) in next st*, rep from * to * 2x and * to ** 1x, tr in same st as first st, ch2, join with tr to first st. {5 sts, 2 3-ch sps on each side; 4 4-ch cnr sps}

R7: ch3 (stch), 4tr over joining tr, *skip 1 st, 2dc in 3-ch sp, dc in next 3 sts, 2dc in 3-ch sp, skip 1 st**, (5tr, ch2, 5tr) in 4-ch sp*, rep from * to * 2x and * to ** 1x, 5tr in same sp as first sts, ch2, join with ss to 3rd ch of stch. Fasten off. {17 sts on each side; 4 2-ch cnr sps}

R8: Attach D with stdg dc to any 2-ch cnr sp, *dc in next 3 sts, htr in next 2 sts, tr in next 7 sts, htr in next 2 sts, dc in next 3 sts**, (dc, ch2, dc) in 2-ch sp*, rep from * to * 2x and * to ** 1x, dc in same sp as first st, ch1, join with dc to first st. {19 sts on each side; 4 2-ch cnr sps}

R9: dc over joining dc, *dc in next 19 sts**, (dc, ch2, dc) in 2-ch sp*, rep from * to * 2x and * to ** 1x, dc in same sp as first st, ch1, join with dc to first st. {21 sts on each side; 4 2-ch cnr sps}

R10: dc over joining dc, *dc in next 21 sts**, (dc, ch2, dc) in 2-ch sp*, rep from * to * 2x and * to ** 1x, dc in same sp as first st, ch2, join with ss to first st. Fasten off. {23 sts on each side; 4 2-ch cnr sps}

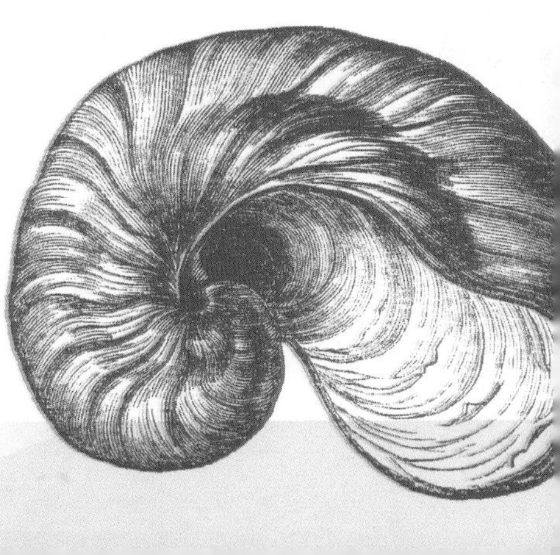

ARAFURA

Located west of the Pacific Ocean
Φ -8.502797, λ 135.399634

Using A, begin with mc.

R1: ch3 (stch), 15tr, join with ss to 3rd ch of stch. {16 sts}

R2: ch3 (stch), tr in previous st, *tr in next st, tr in previous st*, rep from * to * 14x, join with ss to 3rd ch of stch. Fasten off.{32 sts}

R3: Attach B with stdg dtr to any st, dtr in next st, *ch3, dc in next 4 sts, ch3**, dtr in next 4 sts*, rep from * to * 2x and * to ** 1x, dtr in next 2 sts, join with ss to first st. {32 sts, 8 3-ch sps}

R4: ch4 (stch), dtr in next st, *dtr in 3-ch sp, ch4, dc in next 4 sts, ch4, dtr in 3-ch sp**, dtr in next 4 sts*, rep from * to * 2x and * to ** 1x, dtr in next 2 sts, join with ss to 4th ch of stch. Fasten off. {40 sts, 8 4-ch sps}

R5: Attach C with stdg dc to 4th dtr of a group of 6dtr, dc in next 2 sts, *ch3, skip 4-ch sp, dtr in blo of next 4 sts, ch3, skip 4-ch sp, dc in next 3 sts**, ch2, dc in next 3 sts*, rep from * to * 2x and * to ** 1x, ch2, join with ss to first st. Fasten off.
{10 sts, 2 3-ch sps on each side; 4 2-ch cnr sps}

R6: Attach D with stdg tr to any 2-ch cnr sp, tr in same sp, *tr in blo of next 3 sts, tr in each of the next 3 chs, tr in blo of next 4 sts, tr in each of the next 3 chs, tr in blo of next 3 sts**, (2tr, ch2, 2tr) in 2-ch sp*, rep from * to * 2x and * to ** 1x, 2tr in same sp as first sts, ch1, join with dc to first st.
{20 sts on each side; 4 2-ch cnr sps}

R7: dc over joining dc, *dc in next 20 sts**, (dc, ch2, dc) in 2-ch sp*, rep from * to * 2x and * to ** 1x, dc in same sp as first st, ch2, join with ss to first st. Fasten off.
{22 sts on each side; 4 2-ch cnr sps}

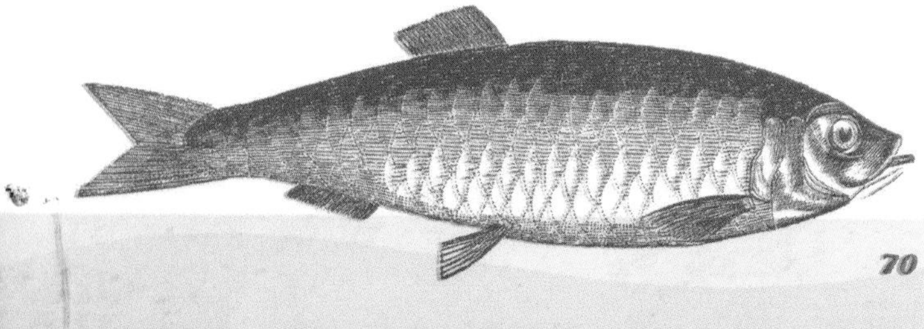

CARPENTARIA

Located in northern Australia
Φ -14.281419, λ 139.327477

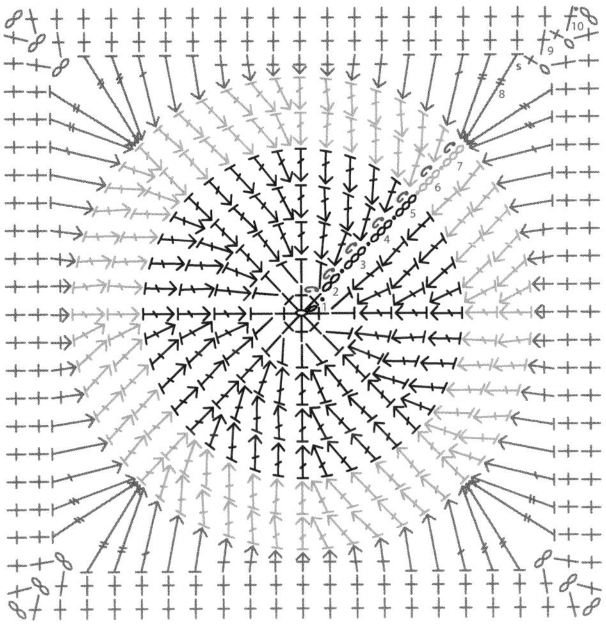

Using A, attach yarn to hook with a slip knot, ch1, work all R1 sts into that ch.

R1: ch1, 8dc, join with ss to first st. {8 sts}

R2: ch2 (stch), htr in same st as ss, 2htr in next 7 sts, join with inv join to first true htr. Fasten off. {16 sts}

R3: Attach A with ss to the lbv of any st, ch3 (stch), tr in same lbv, *tr in lbv of next st**, 2tr in lbv of next st*, rep from * to * 6x and * to ** 1x, cut yarn, join with inv join to first true tr. Fasten off. {24 sts}

R4: Attach B with ss to the lbv of any st, ch3 (stch), tr in same lbv, *tr in lbv of next 2 sts**, 2tr in lbv of next st*, rep from * to * 6x and * to ** 1x, cut yarn, join with inv join to first true tr. Fasten off. {32 sts}

R5: Attach B with ss to the lbv of any st, ch3 (stch), tr in same lbv, *tr in lbv of next 3 sts**, 2tr in lbv of next st*, rep from * to * 6x and * to ** 1x, cut yarn, join with inv join to first true tr. Fasten off. {40 sts}

R6: Attach C with ss to the lbv of any st, ch3 (stch), tr in same lbv, *tr in lbv of next 4 sts**, 2tr in lbv of next st*, rep from * to * 6x and * to ** 1x, cut yarn, join with inv join to first true tr. Fasten off. {48 sts}

R7: Attach C with ss to the lbv of any st, ch3 (stch), tr in same lbv, *tr in lbv of next 5 sts**, 2tr in lbv of next st*, rep from * to * 6x and * to ** 1x, cut yarn, join with inv join to first true tr. Fasten off. {56 sts}

R8: Attach D with a standing dtr to lbv of any st, hdtr in same lbv, *tr in lbv of next st, htr in lbv of next 2 sts, dc in lbv of next 7 sts, htr in lbv of next 2 sts, tr in lbv of next st**, (hdtr, dtr, ch2, dtr, hdtr) in lbv of next st*, rep from * to * 2x and * to ** 1x, (hdtr, dtr) in the same lbv as first sts, ch1, join with dc to first st.
{17 sts on each side; 4 2-ch cnr sps}

R9: dc over joining dc, *dc in next 17 sts**, (dc, ch2, dc) in 2-ch sp*, rep from * to * 2x and * to ** 1x, dc in same sp as first st, ch1, join with dc to first st. {19 sts on each side; 4 2-ch cnr sps}

R10: dc over joining dc, *dc in next 19 sts**, (dc, ch2, dc) in 2-ch sp*, rep from * to * 2x and * to ** 1x, dc in same sp as first st, ch2, join with ss to first st. Fasten off.
{21 sts on each side; 4 2-ch cnr sps}

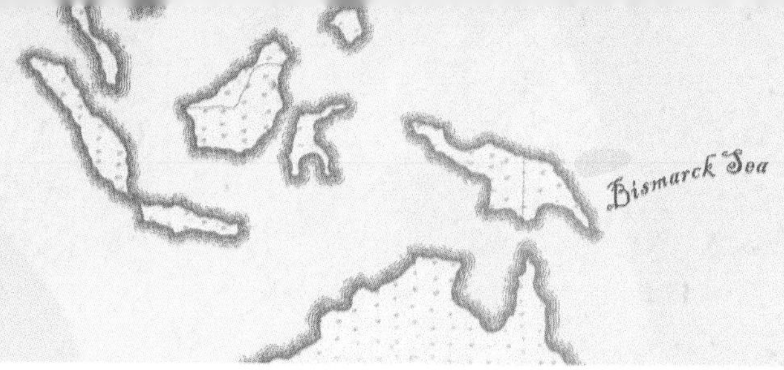

BISMARCK

Located in the southwestern Pacific Ocean
within the nation of Papua New Guinea
Φ -3.697626, λ 148.898400

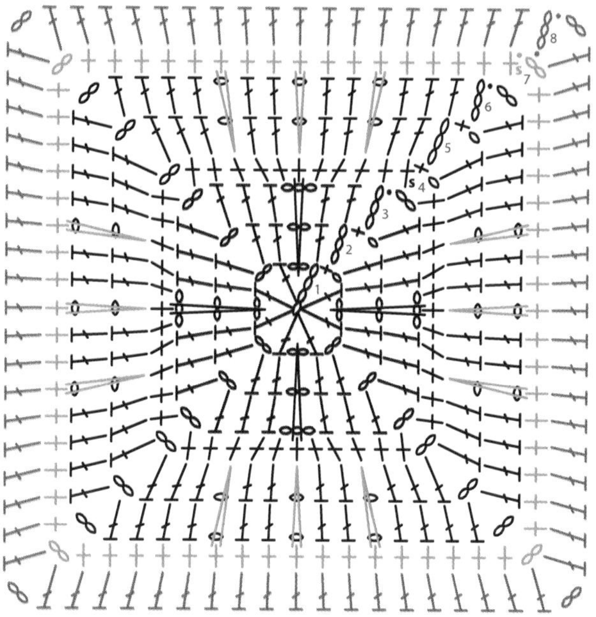

Using A, attach yarn to hook with a slip knot, ch1, work all R1 sts into that ch.

R1: ch3 (stch), *ch2, tr*, rep from * to * 6x, ch1, join with dc to 3rd ch of stch. {8 sts, 8 2-ch-sps}

R2: ch3 (stch), *tr in next st, ch2, skip 2-ch sp, tr in next st**, (tr, ch2, tr) in 2-ch sp*, rep from * to * 2x and * to ** 1x, tr in same sp as first st, ch1, join with dc to 3rd ch of stch.
{4 sts, 1 2-ch sp on each side; 4 2-ch cnr sps}

R3: ch3 (stch), *tr in next 2 sts, ch3, skip 2-ch sp, tr in next 2 sts**, (tr, ch2, tr) in 2-ch sp*, rep from * to * 2x and * to ** 1x, tr in same sp as first st, ch2, join with ss to 3rd ch of stch. Fasten off.
{6 sts, 1 3-ch sp on each side; 4 2-ch cnr sps}

R4: Attach B with stdg dc to any 2-ch cnr sp, *dc in next 3 sts, dc in 3-ch sp, spike dc in 2-ch sp of R1 below, dc in 3-ch sp, dc in next 3 sts**, (dc, ch2, dc) in 2-ch sp*, rep from * to * 2x and * to ** 1x, dc in same sp as first st, ch1, join with dc to first st. {11 sts on each side; 4 2-ch cnr sps}

R5: ch3 (stch), *3x [tr in next 2 sts, ch1, skip 1 st], tr in next 2 sts**, (tr, ch2, tr) in 2-ch sp*, rep from * to * 2x and * to ** 1x, tr in same sp as first st, ch1, join with dc to 3rd ch of stch.
{10 sts, 3 1-ch sps on each side; 4 2-ch cnr sps}

R6: ch3 (stch), *tr in next 3 sts, 2x [ch1, skip 1-ch sp, tr in next 2 sts], ch1, skip 1-ch sp, tr in next 3 sts**, (tr, ch2, tr) in 2-ch sp*, rep from * to * 2x and * to ** 1x, tr in same sp as first st, ch2, join with ss to 3rd ch of stch. Fasten off.
{12 sts, 3 1-ch sps on each side; 4 2-ch cnr sps}

R7: Attach C with stdg dc to any 2-ch cnr sp, *dc in next 4 sts, 2x [spike dc in skipped st of R4 below, dc in next 2 sts], spike dc in skipped st of R4 below, dc in next 4 sts**, (dc, ch2, dc) in 2-ch sp*, rep from * to * 2x and * to ** 1x, dc in same sp as first st, ch2, join with ss to first st. Fasten off. {17 sts on each side; 4 2-ch cnr sps}

R8: Attach D with ss to any 2-ch cnr sp, ch3 (stch), *tr in next 17 sts**, (tr, ch2, tr) in 2-ch sp*, rep from * to * 2x and * to ** 1x, tr in same sp as first st, ch2, join with ss to 3rd ch of stch. Fasten off. {19 sts on each side; 4 2-ch cnr sps}

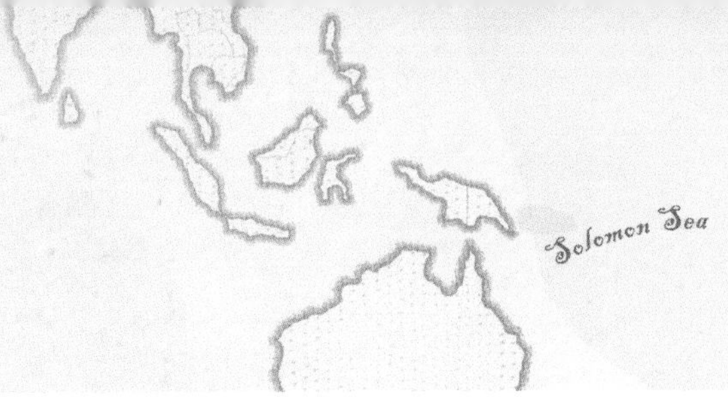

SOLOMON

Located in the Pacific Ocean between Papua New Guinea and the Solomon Islands
Φ -8.000000, λ 155.000000

Using A, begin with mc.

R1: ch3 (stch), 15tr, join with ss to 3rd ch of stch. Fasten off. {16 sts}

R2: Attach B with stdg dc to any st, *ch2, dc in next st*, rep from * to * 14x, ch2, join with ss to first st. {16 sts, 16 2-ch sps}

R3: *(dc, htr, tr, ch2, tr, htr, dc) in 2-ch sp**, ch1, skip (1 st, 2-ch sp and 1 st)*, rep from * to * 6x and * to ** 1x, ch1, join with ss to first st. Fasten off. {48 sts, 8 1-ch sps, 8 2-ch sps}

R4: Attach C with stdg hdtr to any 2-ch sp of R2 over 1-ch sp of R3, *ch2, skip 3 sts, dc in 2-ch sp, ch2, skip 3 sts**, hdtr over 1-ch sp of R3 in 2-ch sp of R2*, rep from * to * 6x and * to ** 1x, join with ss to first st. {16 sts, 16 2-ch sps}

R5: dc in same st as ss, *2dc in 2-ch sp**, dc in next st*, rep from * to * 14x and * to ** 1x, join with ss to first st. {48 sts}

R6: ch3 (stch), *ch2, skip 1 st**, tr in next st*, rep from * to * 22x and * to ** 1x, join with ss to 3rd ch of stch. Fasten off. {24 sts, 24 2-ch sps}

R7: Attach D with stdg tr to any st, *skip 2-ch sp, 4x [dc in next st, 2dc in 2-ch sp], dc in next st, skip 2-ch sp**, (tr, ch4, tr) in next st*, rep from * to * 2x and * to ** 1x, tr in same st as first st, ch1, join with tr to first st.
{15 sts on each side; 4 4-ch cnr sps}

R8: 2dc over joining tr, *dc in next 15 sts**, (2dc, ch2, 2dc) in 4-ch sp*, rep from * to * 2x and * to ** 1x, 2dc in same sp as first sts, ch1, join with dc to first st.
{19 sts on each side; 4 2-ch cnr sps}

R9: dc over joining dc, *9x [ch1, skip 1 st, dc in next st], ch1, skip 1 st**, (dc, ch2, dc) in 2-ch sp*, rep from * to * 2x and * to ** 1x, dc in same sp as first st, ch1, join with dc to first st.
{11 sts, 10 1-ch sps on each side; 4 2-ch cnr sps}

R10: dc over joining dc, *10x [dc in next st, dc in 1-ch sp], dc in next st**, (dc, ch2, dc) in 2-ch sp*, rep from * to * 2x and * to ** 1x, dc in same sp as first st, ch2, join with ss to first st. Fasten off.
{23 sts on each side; 4 2-ch cnr sps}

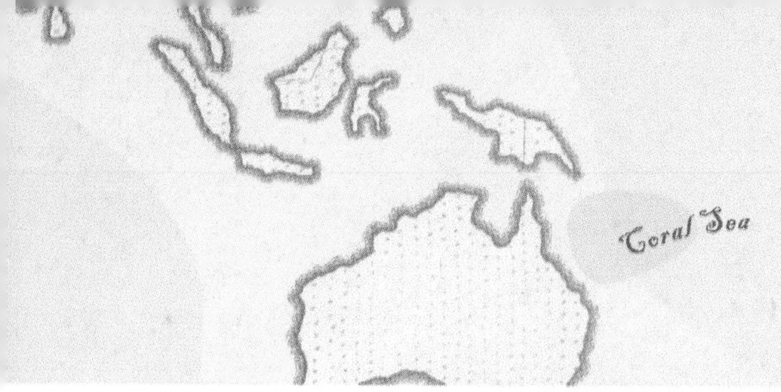

CORAL

Located off the northeast coast of Australia
Φ -18.379548, λ 156.772585

Using A, attach yarn to hook with a slip knot, ch1, work all R1 sts into that ch.

R1: ch1, 8dc, join with ss to first st. {8 sts}

R2: dc in same st as ss, *ch4, skip 1 st**, dc in next st*, rep from * to * 2x and * to ** 1x, join with ss to first st. {4 sts, 4 4-ch sps}

R3: ch3 (stch), 4tr in same st as ss, *dc in 4-ch sp**, 5tr in next st*, rep from * to * 2x and * to ** 1x, join with ss to 3rd ch of stch. Fasten off. {1 st on each side; 4 5-st cnrs}

R4: Attach B with stdg dc to middle st of any 5-st cnr, *ch4, skip 2 sts, tr in next st, ch4, skip 2 sts**, dc in next st*, rep from * to * 2x and * to ** 1x, join with ss to first st. {8 sts, 8 4-ch sps}

R5: ch3 (stch), 4tr in same st as ss, *dc in 4-ch sp**, 5tr in next st*, rep from * to * 6x and * to ** 1x, join with ss to 3rd ch of stch. Fasten off. {48 sts}

R6: Attach C with stdg dc to middle st of any 5-st group, *ch3, skip 2 sts, tr in next st, ch3, skip 2 sts**, dc in next st*, rep from * to * 6x and * to ** 1x, join with ss to first st. {16 sts, 16 3-ch sps}

R7: ch3 (stch), 4tr in same st as ss, *dc in 3-ch sp**, 5tr in next st*, rep from * to * 14x and * to ** 1x, join with ss to 3rd ch of stch. Fasten off. {96 sts}

R8: Attach D with stdg tr to middle st of any 5-st group, *3x [ch2, skip 2 sts, tr in next st, ch2, skip 2 sts, dc in next st], ch2, skip 2 sts, tr in next st, ch2, skip 2 sts**, (tr, ch2, tr) in next st*, rep from * to * 2x and * to ** 1x, tr in same st as first st, ch1, join with dc to first st. {9 sts, 8 2-ch sps on each side; 4 2-ch cnr sps}

R9: 2dc over joining dc, *8x [dc in next st, dc in 2-ch sp], dc in next st**, (2dc, ch2, 2dc) in 2-ch sp*, rep from * to * 2x and * to ** 1x, 2dc in same sp as first sts, ch2, join with ss to first st. Fasten off. {21 sts on each side; 4 2-ch cnr sps}

TASMAN

Located in the South Pacific Ocean
Φ -38.575657, λ 161.584295

Using A, ch 12, join with ss to first ch over the top 2 strands of the first ch.

R1: ch3 (stch), tr in same ch as ss, 2tr in next 11 chs, working over the top 2 loops of the chs, join with ss to 3rd ch of stch. Fasten off. {24 sts}

R2: Attach B with ss to any st, *ch5, skip 1 st, ss into next st*, rep from * to * 10x, ch2, join with tr to same st as ss attaching B. {12 5-ch sps, 12 ss}

R3: dc over joining tr, *skip 1 st, (dc, htr, tr, ch1, tr, htr, dc) in 5-ch sp, skip 1 st**, (dc, ch2, dc) in 5-ch sp*, rep from * to * 4x and * to ** 1x, dc in same sp as first st, ch2, join with ss to first st. Fasten off. {48 sts, 6 1-ch sps, 6 2-ch sps}

R4: Attach C with stdg tr to any 2-ch sp, *ch3, skip 4 sts, dc in 1-ch sp, ch3, skip 4 sts**, (tr, ch2, tr) in 2-ch sp*, rep from * to * 4x and * to ** 1x, tr in same sp as first st, ch1, join with dc to first st. {18 sts, 12 3-ch sps, 6 2-ch sps}

R5: dc over joining dc, *dc in next st, 3dc in 3-ch sp, skip 1 st, 3dc in 3-ch sp, dc in next st**, 2dc in 2-ch sp*, rep from * to * 4x and * to ** 1x, dc in same sp as first st, join with ss to first st. Fasten off. {60 sts}

R6: Attach D with stdg tr to any st, *tr in next 2 sts, htr in next 3 sts, dc in next 4 sts, htr in next 3 sts, tr in next 2 sts**, (tr, ch3, tr) in next st*, rep from * to * 2x and * to ** 1x, tr in same st as first st, ch1, join with htr to first st.
{16 sts on each side; 4 3-ch cnr sps}

R7: ch3 (stch), ch1, tr over joining htr, *tr in next st, htr in next 2 sts, dc in next 10 sts, htr in next 2 sts, tr in next st**, (2x [tr, ch1], tr) in 3-ch sp*, rep from * to * 2x and * to ** 1x, tr in same sp as first sts, ch1, join with ss to 3rd ch of stch.
{16 sts on each side; 4 (tr, ch1, tr, ch1, tr) cnrs}

R8: dc in same st as ss, *dc in 1-ch sp, dc in next 18 sts, dc in 1-ch sp**, (dc, ch2, dc) in next st*, rep from * to * 2x and * to ** 1x, dc in same st as first st, ch1, join with dc to first st.
{22 sts on each side; 4 2-ch cnr sps}

R9: dc over joining dc, *dc in next 22 sts**, (dc, ch2, dc) in 2-ch sp*, rep from * to * 2x and * to ** 1x, dc in same sp as first st, ch2, join with ss to first st. Fasten off.
{24 sts on each side; 4 2-ch cnr sps}

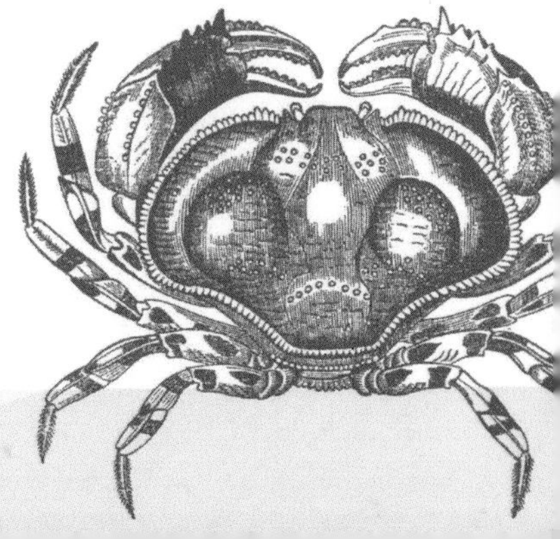

SOMOV

Part of the Southern Ocean, near Antarctica
Φ -69.754633, λ 168.622170

Using A, begin with mc.

R1: ch3 (stch), tr, *ch2**, 2tr*, rep from * to * 6x and * to ** 1x, join with ss to 3rd ch of stch. {16 sts, 8 2-ch sps}

R2: ch3 (stch), tr in same st as ss, 2tr in next st, *ch1, skip 2-ch sp**, 2tr in next 2 sts*, rep from * to * 6x and * to ** 1x, join with ss to 3rd ch of stch. Fasten off. {32 sts, 8 1-ch sps}

R3: Attach B with stdg dc to a st after any 1-ch sp, dc in next 3 sts, *puff in 2 ch-sp of R1**, dc in next 4 sts*, rep from * to * 6x and * to ** 1x, join with ss to first st. {40 sts}

R4: ch3 (stch), tr in next 39 sts, join with ss to 3rd ch of stch. {40 sts}

R5: dc in same st as ss, dc in next 39 sts, join with ss to first st. {40 sts}

R6: ch3 (stch), tr in same st as ss, *ch1, skip 1 st**, 2tr in next st*, rep from * to * 18x and * to ** 1x, join with ss to 3rd ch of stch. Fasten off. {40 sts, 20 1-ch sps}

R7: Attach C with stdg dc to a st after any 1-ch sp, dc in next st, *puff in skipped st of R5**, dc in next 2 sts*, rep from * to * 18x and * to ** 1x, join with ss to first st. Fasten off. {60 sts}

R8: Attach D with stdg dtr to any st, dtr in same st, *skip 1 st, 3tr in next st, skip 1 st, dc in next 8 sts, skip 1 st, 3tr in next st, skip 1 st**, 3dtr in next st*, rep from * to * 2x and * to ** 1x, dtr in same st as first sts, join with ss to first st. {14 sts in each side; 4 3-st cnrs}

R9: dc in same st as ss, *dc in next 16 sts**, (dc, ch2, dc) in next st*, rep from * to * 2x and * to ** 1x, dc in same st as first st, ch1, join with dc to first st. {18 sts on each side; 4 2-ch cnr sps}

R10: dc over joining dc, *dc in next 18 sts**, (dc, ch2, dc) in 2-ch sp*, rep from * to * 2x and * to ** 1x, dc in same sp as first st, ch2, join with ss to first st. Fasten off. {20 sts on each side; 4 2-ch cnr sps}

D'URVILLE

Located in the Southern Ocean, near Antarctica
Φ -67.716112, λ 148.942698

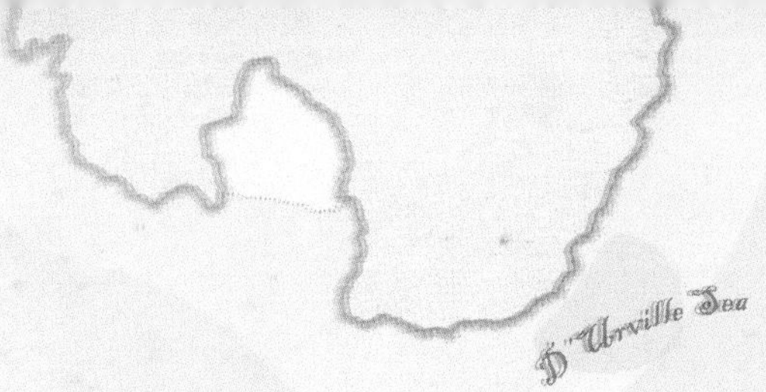

★ *Special Stitch: modified treble (mtr)- a normal tr with an extra step to anchor the top sts to the square. Begin your tr as normal, yo, insert hook in ch sp, pull a loop to the front, yo, pull through 2 loops on hook, insert your hook in the st behind from the previous round and pull a loop to the front and through both loops on the hook.*

Using A, attach yarn to hook.

R1: ch1, 12dc, join with ss to first st. {12 sts}

R2: ch3 (stch), 2tr in same st as ss, *tr2tog in blo of next 2 sts**, 5tr in next st*, rep from * to * 2x and * to ** 1x, 2tr in same st as first sts, join with ss to 3rd ch of stch. {24 sts}

R3: dc in same st as ss, *ch2, skip 2 sts of R2, tr in flo of next 2 sts of R1, ch2, skip 3 sts of R2**, dc in next st*, rep from * to * 2x and * to ** 1x, join with ss to first st.
{2 sts, 2 2-ch sps on each side; 4 1-st cnrs}

R4: ch3 (stch), 4tr in same st as ss, *skip (R3 sts and ch sps), tr in next 5 sts of R2**, 5tr in next st of R3*, rep from * to * 2x and * to **, join with ss to 3rd ch of stch. Fasten off.
{5 sts on each side; 4 5-st cnrs}

R5: Attach B with stdg dc to any middle st of a 5-st cnr, *ch2, skip 2 sts of R4, 2tr in 2-ch sp of R3, ch2, skip 2 sts of R3, 2tr in 2-ch sp of R3, ch2, skip 2 sts of R4**, dc in next st of R4*, rep from * to * 2x and * to ** 1x, join with ss to first st.
{4 sts, 3 2-ch sps on each side; 4 1-st cnrs}

R6: ch3 (stch), 4tr in same st as ss, *skip (R5 sts and ch sps), tr in next 9 sts of R4**, 5tr in next st of R5*, rep from * to * 2x and * to **, join with ss to 3rd ch of stch. Fasten off.
{9 sts on each side; 4 5-st cnrs}

R7: Attach C with stdg dc to any middle st of a 5-st cnr, *ch2, skip 2 sts of R6, 2x [2tr in 2-ch sp of R5, ch2, skip 2 sts of R5], 2tr in 2-ch sp of R5, ch2, skip 2 sts of R6**, dc in next st of R6*, rep from * to * 2x and * to ** 1x, join with ss to first st. {6 sts, 4 2-ch sps on each side; 4 1-st cnrs}

R8: ch3 (stch), 4tr in same st as ss, *skip (R7 sts and ch sps), tr in next 12 sts of R6, 2tr in next st**, 5tr in next st of R7*, rep from * to * 2x and * to **, join with ss to 3rd ch of stch. Fasten off.
{14 sts on each side; 4 5-st cnrs}

R9: Attach D with stdg dc to any middle st of a 5-st cnr, *dc in next 2 sts of R8, 4x [2mtr in 2-ch sps of R7 and next sts of R8, dc in next 2 sts of R8]**, (dc, ch2, dc) in next st of R8*, rep from * to * 2x and * to ** 1x, dc in same st as first st, ch1, join with dc to first st.
{20 sts on each side; 4 2-ch cnr sps}

R10: ch3 (stch), *tr in next 20 sts**, (tr, ch2, tr) in next st*, rep from * to * 2x and * to ** 1x, tr in same sp as first st, ch2, join with ss to 3rd ch of stch. Fasten off.
{22 sts on each side; 4 2-ch cnr sps}

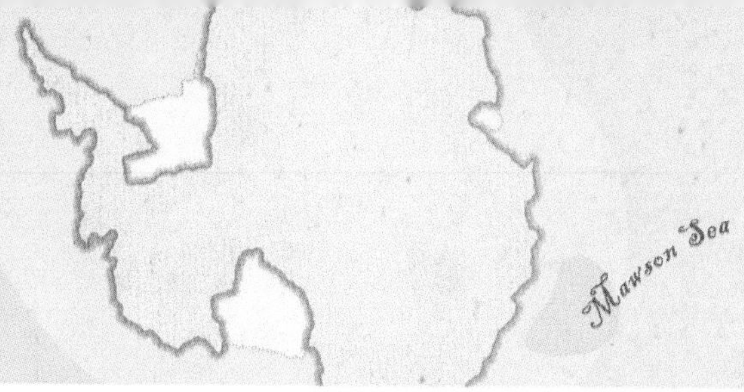

MAWSON

Located off the east coast of Antarctica
Φ -64.623882, λ 111.445822

Using A, attach yarn to hook with a slip knot, ch1, work all R1 sts into that ch.

R1: ch3 (stch), 11tr, join with ss to 3rd ch of stch. {12 sts}

R2: ch3 (stch), *fptr around previous st**, tr in next st*, rep from * to * 10x and * to ** 1x, join with ss to 3rd ch of stch. Fasten off. {24 sts}

R3: Attach B with stdg tr to any tr (not fp), tr in same st, *fptr around previous fp st, tr in next st**, 2tr in next st*, rep from * to * 10x and * to ** 1x, join with ss to first st. {48 sts}

R4: ch3 (stch), tr in next 3 sts, *fptr around previous fp st**, tr in next 4 sts*, rep from * to * 10x and * to ** 1x, join with ss to 3rd ch of stch. Fasten off. {60 sts}

R5: Attach C with stdg tr to any st after a fp st, *fptr around previous fp st**, tr in next 5 sts* rep from * to * 10x and * to ** 1x, tr in next 4 sts, join with ss to first st. {72 sts}

R6: ch1 (stch), dc in next 71 sts, join with inv join to first st. Fasten off. {72 sts}

R7: Attach C with stdg bpdc around next fp st of R5, *ch5**, skip 5 sts, bpdc around next fp st of R5*, rep from * to * 10x and * to ** 1x, join with ss to first st. Fasten off. {12 sts, 12 5-ch sps}

R8: Attach D with stdg dtr to any st, hdtr in same st, *(3tr, 2htr) in 5-ch sp, htr in next st, 5dc in 5-ch sp, htr in next st, (2htr, 3tr) in 5-ch sp**, (hdtr, dtr, hdtr) in next st*, rep from * to * 2x and * to ** 1x, hdtr in same st as first sts, join with ss to first st. {17 sts on each side; 4 3-st cnrs}

R9: dc in same st as ss, *dc in next 19 sts**, (dc, ch2, dc) in next st*, rep from * to * 2x and * to ** 1x, dc in same st as first st, ch1, join with dc to first st. {21 sts on each side; 4 2-ch cnr sps}

R10: dc over joining dc, *dc in next 21 sts**, (dc, ch2, dc) in 2-ch sp*, rep from * to * 2x and * to ** 1x, dc in same sp as first st, ch2, join with ss to first st. Fasten off.
{23 sts on each side; 4 2-ch cnr sps}

COOPERATION

Part of the Southern Ocean, near Antarctica
Φ -67.822509, λ 70.274498

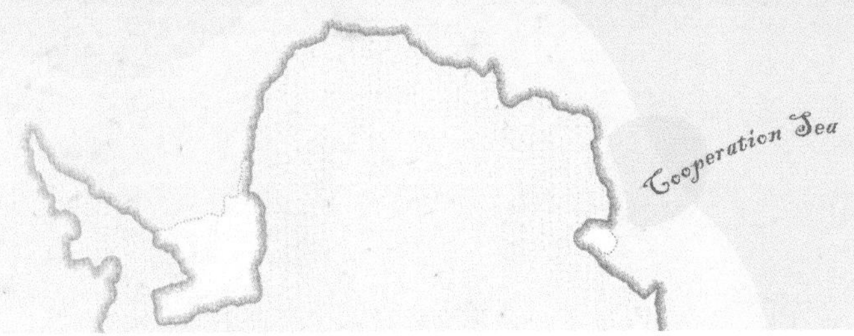

Using A, attach yarn to hook with a slip knot, ch1, work all R1 sts into that ch.

R1: ch3 (stch), *ch1, tr*, rep from * to * 10x, join with dc to 3rd ch of stch. {12 sts, 12 1-ch sps}

R2: ch3 (stch), tr over joining dc, *ch1, skip 1 st, puff in 1-ch sp, ch1, skip 1 st**, 3tr in 1-ch sp*, rep from * to * 4x and * to ** 1x, tr in same sp as first sts, join with ss to 3rd ch of stch. Fasten off. {24, 12 1-ch sps}

R3: Attach B with stdg dc to first tr of a 3-tr group, dc in next 2 sts, *dc in 1-ch sp, skip 1 st, dc in 1-ch sp**, dc in next 3 sts*, rep from * to * 4x and * to ** 1x, join with ss to first st. {30 sts}

R4: dc in same st as ss, *ch1**, dc in next st*, rep from * to * 28x and * to ** 1x, join with ss to first st. {30 sts, 30 1-ch sps}

R5: dc in same st as ss, *dc in 1-ch sp**, dc in next st*, rep from * to * 28x and * to ** 1x, join with ss to first st. Fasten off. {60 sts}

R6: Attach C with stdg dtr to any st, 2x [ch1, dtr] in same st, *skip 3 sts, dc in next 8 sts, skip 3 sts**, (4x [dtr, ch1], dtr) in next st*, rep from * to * 2x and * to ** 1x, 2x [dtr, ch1] in same st as first sts, join with ss to first st.
{12 sts, 4 1-ch sps on each side; 4 1-st cnrs}

R7: dc in same st as ss, *dc in 1-ch sp, dc in next st, dc in 1-ch sp, dc in next 10 sts, dc in 1-ch sp, dc in next st, dc in 1-ch sp**, (dc, ch2, dc) in next st*, rep from * to * 2x and * to ** 1x, dc in same st as first st, ch2, join with ss to first st. Fasten off. {18 sts on each side; 4 2-ch cnr sps}

R8: Attach D with stdg tr to any 2-ch cnr sp, *ch1, skip 1 st, puff in next st, ch1, skip 2 sts, 3tr in next st, ch1, skip 2 sts, puff in next st, ch1, tr2tog over next 2 sts, ch1, puff in next st, ch1, skip 2 sts, 3tr in next st, ch1, skip 2 sts, puff in next st, ch1, skip 1 st**, (tr, ch2, tr) in 2-ch sp*, rep from * to * 2x and * to ** 1x, tr in same sp as first st, ch1, join with dc to first st.
{13 sts, 8 1-ch sps on each side; 4 2-ch cnr sps}

R9: dc over joining dc, *dc in next st, dc in 1-ch sp, skip 1 st, dc in 1-ch sp, dc in next 3 sts, dc in 1-ch sp, skip 1 st, dc in 1-ch sp, dc in next st, dc in 1-ch sp, skip 1 st, dc in 1-ch sp, dc in next 3 sts, dc in 1-ch sp, skip 1 st, dc in 1-ch sp, dc in next st**, (dc, ch2, dc) in 2-ch sp*, rep from * to * 2x and * to ** 1x, dc in same sp as first st, ch1, join with dc to first st.
{19 sts on each side; 4 2-ch cnr sps}

R10: dc over joining dc, *dc in next 19 sts**, (dc, ch2, dc) in 2-ch sp*, rep from * to * 2x and * to ** 1x, dc in same sp as first st, ch2, join with ss to first st. Fasten off.
{21 sts on each side; 4 2-ch cnr sps}

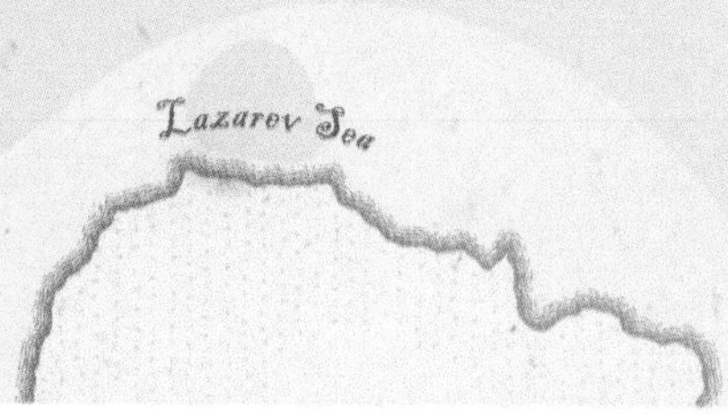

LAZAREV

Located in the Southern Ocean, near Antarctica
Φ -69.509921, λ -6.152555

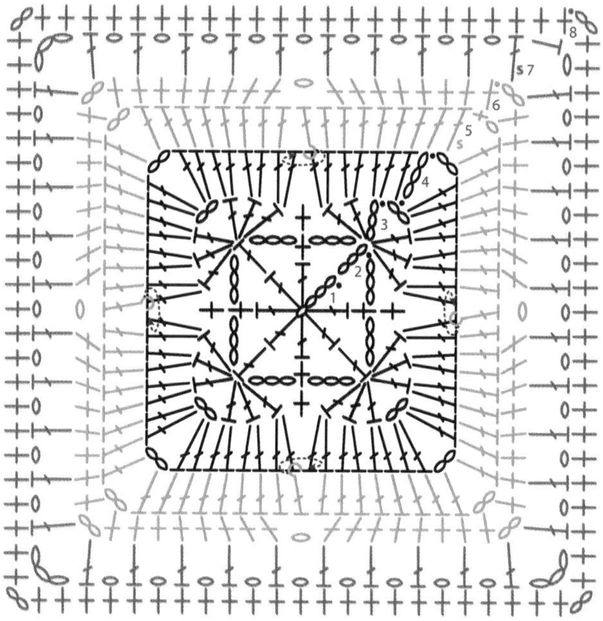

Using A, attach yarn to hook with a slip knot, ch1, work all R1 sts into that ch.

R1: ch3 (stch), 7tr, join with ss to 3rd ch of stch. {8 sts}

R2: ch3 (stch), *ch3, dc in next st, ch3**, tr in next st*, rep from * to * 2x and * to ** 1x, join with ss to 3rd ch of stch. {8 sts, 8 3-ch sps}

R3: ch3 (stch), 2tr in same st as ss, *skip 3-ch sp, dc in next st, skip 3-ch sp**, (3tr, ch2, 3tr) in next st*, rep from * to * 2x and * to ** 1x, 3tr in same st as first sts, ch2, join with ss to 3rd ch of stch. Fasten off.
{7 sts on each side; 4 2-ch cnr sps}

R4: Attach B with ss to any 2-ch cnr sp, ch3 (stch), tr in same sp, *2tr in next 3 sts, skip 1 st, 2tr in next 3 sts**, (2tr, ch2, 2tr) in 2-ch sp*, rep from * to * 2x and * to ** 1x, 2tr in same sp as first sts, ch2, join with ss to 3rd ch of stch. Fasten off. {16 sts on each side; 4 2-ch cnr sps}

R5: Attach C with stdg tr to any 2-ch cnr sp, *tr in next 7 sts, fptr around next 2 sts at the same time, tr in next 7 sts**, (tr, ch2, tr) in 2-ch sp*, rep from * to * 2x and * to ** 1x, tr in same sp as first st, ch1, join with dc to first st.
{17 sts on each side; 4 2-ch cnr sps}

R6: dc over joining dc, *dc in next 7 sts, ch1, skip next 3 sts, dc in next 7 sts**, (dc, ch2, dc) in 2-ch sp*, rep from * to * 2x and * to ** 1x, dc in same sp as first st, ch2, join with ss to first st. Fasten off.
{16 sts, 1 1-ch sp on each side; 4 2-ch cnr sps}

R7: Attach D with stdg tr to any 2-ch cnr sp, *4x [ch1, skip 1 st, tr in next st], ch1, skip 1-ch sp, 4x [tr in next st, ch1, skip 1 st]**, (tr, ch3, tr) in 2-ch sp*, rep from * to * 2x and * to ** 1x, tr in same sp as first st, ch1, join with htr to first st.
{10 sts, 9 1-ch sps on each side; 4 3-ch cnr sps}

R8: 2dc over joining htr, *9x [dc in next st, dc in 1-ch sp], dc in next st**, (2dc, ch2, 2dc) in 3-ch sp*, rep from * to * 2x and * to ** 1x, 2dc in same sp as first sts, ch2, join with ss to first st. Fasten off. {23 sts on each side; 4 2-ch cnr sps}

WEDDELL

Part of the Southern Ocean near Antarctica
Φ -73.307676, λ -42.704351

Using A, attach yarn to hook with a slip knot, ch1, work all R1 sts into that ch.

R1: ch3 (stch), 11tr, join with ss to 3rd ch of stch. {12 sts}

R2: ch3 (stch), *skip 1 st**, (tr, ch3, tr) in next st*, rep from * to * 4x and * to ** 1x, tr in same st as first st, ch1, join with htr to 3rd ch of stch. {12 sts, 6 3-ch sps}

R3: dc over joining htr, *ch1, 5tr between next 2 sts, ch1**, dc in 3-ch sp*, rep from * to * 4x and * to ** 1x, join with ss to first st. Fasten off. {36 sts, 12 1-ch sps}

R4: Attach B with stdg dc to any dc, *dc in 1-ch sp, ch3, skip next 5 sts, dc in 1-ch sp**, dc in next st*, rep from * to * 4x and * to ** 1x, join with ss to first st. {18 sts, 6 3-ch sps}

R5: dc in same st as ss, dc in next st, *ch1, 7tr in 3-ch sp, ch1**, dc in next 3 sts*, rep from * to * 4x and * to ** 1x, dc in next st, join with ss to first st. Fasten off. {60 sts, 12 1-ch sps}

R6: Attach C with stdg dc to middle st of any 3-st group, dc in next st, *dc in 1-ch sp, ch5, skip next 7 sts, dc in 1-ch sp**, dc in next 3 sts*, rep from * to * 4x and * to ** 1x, dc in next st, join with ss to first st. {30 sts, 6 5-ch sps}

R7: dc in same st as ss, dc in next 2 sts, *ch1, 9tr in 5-ch sp, ch1**, dc in next 5 sts*, rep from * to * 4x and * to ** 1x, dc in next 2 sts, join with ss to first st. Fasten off. {84 sts, 12 1-ch sps}

R8: Attach D with stdg dc to middle st of any 5-st group, dc in next 2 sts, *dc in 1-ch sp, ch7, skip next 9 sts, dc in 1-ch sp**, dc in next 5 sts*, rep from * to * 4x and * to ** 1x, dc in next 2 sts, join with ss to first st. {42 sts, 6 7-ch sps}

R9: ch3 (stch), tr in next 3 sts, *5htr in 7-ch sp**, tr in next 7 sts*, rep from * to * 4x and * to ** 1x, tr in next 3 sts, join with ss to 3rd ch of stch. {72 sts}

R10: ch3 (stch), 2tr in same st as ss, *skip 2 sts, dc in next 13 sts, skip 2 sts**, (3tr, ch2, 3tr) in next st*, rep from * to * 2x and * to ** 1x, 3tr in same st as first sts, ch1, join with dc to 3rd ch of stch. {19 sts on each side; 4 2-ch cnr sps}

R11: dc over joining dc, *dc in next 2 sts, htr in next 2 sts, dc in next 11 sts, htr in next 2 sts, dc in next 2 sts**, (dc, ch2, dc) in 2-ch sp*, rep from * to * 2x and * to ** 1x, dc in same sp as first st, ch2, join with ss to first st. Fasten off. {21 sts on each side; 4 2-ch cnr sps}

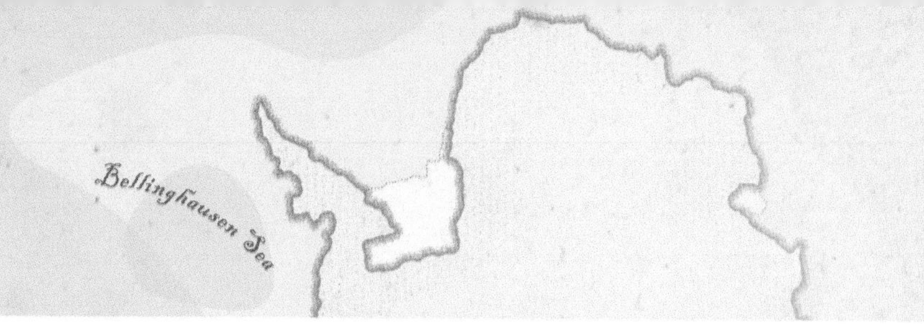

BELLINGHAUSEN

Located along the west side of the
Antarctic Peninsula
Φ -68.656555, λ 283.045739

Using A, begin with mc.

R1: ch3 (stch), 15tr, join with ss to 3rd ch of stch. {16 sts}

R2: ch3 (stch), fptr around st ss'd into, fptr around next st, *ch3, fptr around next 2 sts, tr in same st last fp st was worked around**, ch2, tr in next st, fptr around same st last st was worked into, fptr around next st*, rep from * to * 2x and * to ** 1x, ch2, join with ss to 3rd ch of stch. Fasten off.
{6 sts, 1 3-ch sp on each side; 4 2-ch cnr sps}

R3: Attach B with stdg tr to any 2-ch cnr sp, *fptr around next 3 sts, ch4, skip 3-ch sp, fptr around next 3 sts**, (tr, ch2, tr) in 2-ch sp*, rep from * to * 2x and * to ** 1x, tr in same sp as first st, ch1, join with dc to first st.
{8 sts, 1 4-ch sp on each side; 4 2-ch cnr sps}

R4: ch3 (stch), *fptr around next 4 sts, ch5, skip 4-ch sp, fptr around next 4 sts**, (tr, ch2, tr) in 2-ch sp*, rep from * to * 2x and * to ** 1x, tr in same sp as first st, ch1, join with dc to 3rd ch of stch.
{10 sts, 1 5-ch sp on each side; 4 2-ch cnr sps}

R5: ch3 (stch), *fptr around next 5 sts, ch2, dc over ch loops of previous 3 rnds, ch2, fptr around next 5 sts**, (tr, ch2, tr) in 2-ch sp*, rep from * to * 2x and * to ** 1x, tr in same sp as first st, ch1, join with dc to 3rd ch of stch.
{13 sts, 2 2-ch sps on each side; 4 2-ch cnr sps}

R6: ch3 (stch), *fptr around next 3 sts, fptr3tog around next 3 sts, ch2, skip 2-ch sp, tr in next st, ch2, skip 2-ch sp, fptr3tog around next 3 sts, fptr around next 3 sts**, (tr, ch2, tr) in 2-ch sp*, rep from * to * 2x and * to ** 1x, tr in same sp as first st, ch1, join with dc to 3rd ch of stch.
{11 sts, 2 2-ch sps on each side; 4 2-ch cnr sps}

R7: dc over joining dc, *fpdc around next 5 sts, 2dc in 2-ch sp, dc in next st, 2dc in 2-ch sp, fpdc around next 5 sts**, (dc, ch2, dc) in 2-ch sp*, rep from * to * 2x and * to ** 1x, dc in same sp as first st, ch2, join with ss to first st. Fasten off.
{17 sts on each side; 4 2-ch cnr sps}

R8: Attach C with ss to any 2-ch cnr sp, ch3 (stch), *tr in next st, tr in next 5 sts of R6 behind R7 sts, htr in next 5 sts, tr in next 5 sts of R6 behind R7 sts, tr in next st**, (tr, ch2, tr) in 2-ch sp*, rep from * to * 2x and * to ** 1x, tr in same sp as first st, ch2, join with ss to 3rd ch of stch . Fasten off. {19 sts on each side; 4 2-ch cnr sps}

R9: Attach D with stdg dc in any 2-ch cnr sp, *dc in next 19 sts**, (dc, ch2, dc) in 2-ch sp*, rep from * to * 2x and * to ** 1x, dc in same sp as first st, ch1, join with dc to first st.
{21 sts on each side; 4 2-ch cnr sps}

R10: dc over joining dc, *dc in next 21sts**, (dc, ch2, dc) in 2-ch sp*, rep from * to * 2x and * to ** 1x, dc in same sp as first st, ch2, join with ss to first st. Fasten off.
{23 sts on each side; 4 2-ch cnr sps}

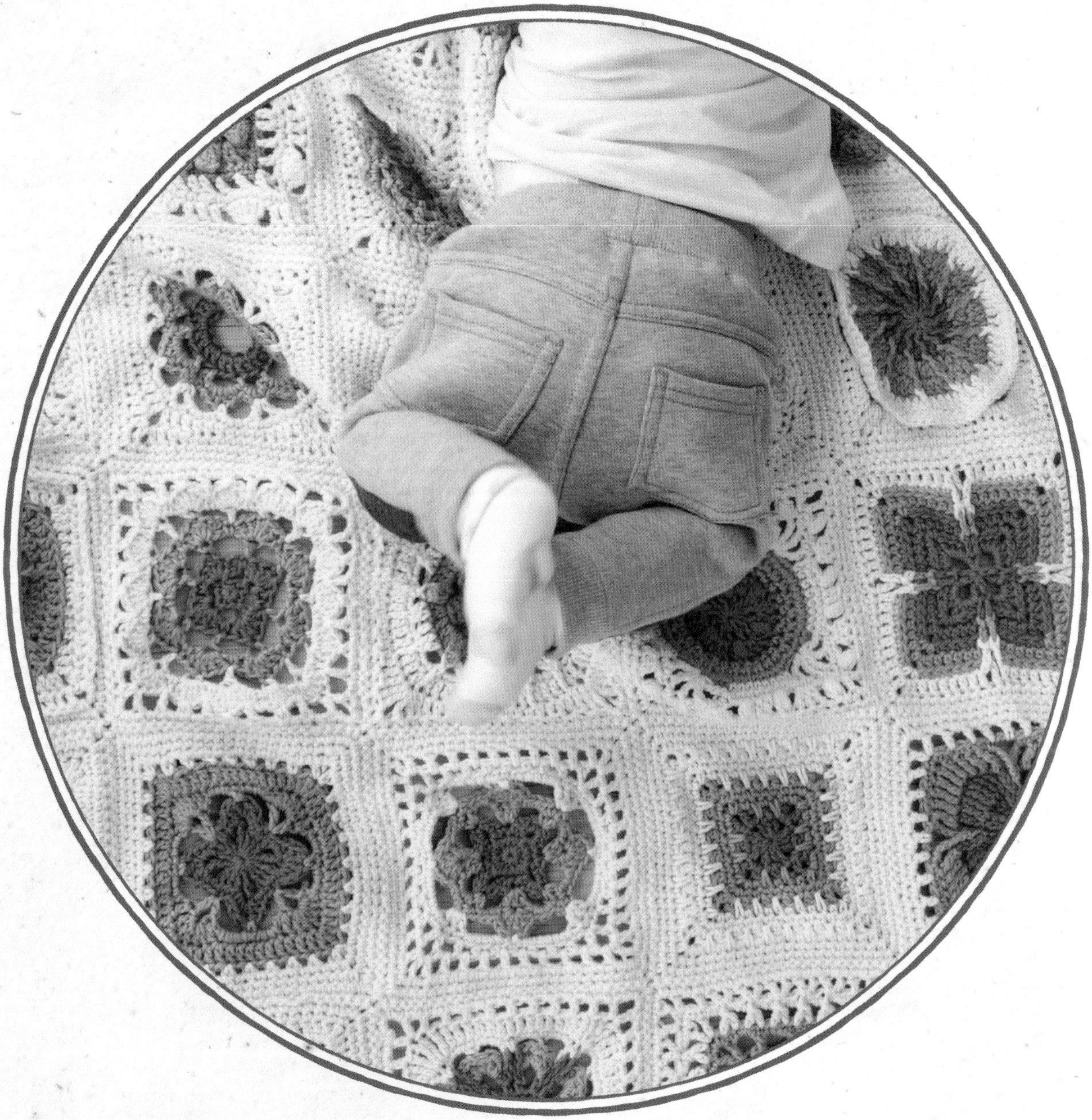

Glossary

This list describes all the abbreviations, stitches and techniques used in this book. Abbreviations are simply words that have been shortened. Stitches are complete stitches you will need to know. Techniques describe how particular stitches are made. Rather than explain all the variations resulting from combinations of stitches and techniques, each abbreviation, stitch and technique is described on its own. You will use them all, in different combinations, to create your squares.

Symbols used in the charts are also shown, where applicable.

Abbreviations			
	cnr/s	corner/s	
	R	round	
	rep	repeat	
	sp/s	space/s	
	st/s	stitch/es	
	stch	starting chain	Used in place of the first st in a round. Is included in stitch count.
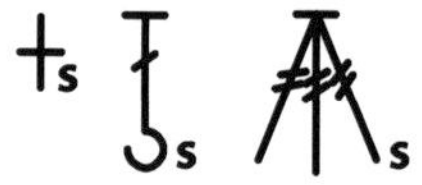	stdg	standing	Attach yarn to your hook with a slip knot then work the stitch indicated as normal. Can be any stitch.
	yo	yarn over	Wrap yarn over hook from back to front.
Stitches			
•	ss	slip stitch	Insert hook into st or sp indicated, yo and pull through st or sp and loop on hook.
o	ch	chain	Yarn over, pull through loop on hook.
+	dc	double crochet	Insert hook into st or sp indicated, yo, pull loop to front, yo, pull through both loops on hook.
T	htr	half treble crochet	Wrap yarn around hook, insert hook into st or sp indicated, yo, pull loop to front (3 loops on hook), yo, pull through all 3 loops on hook.
	tr	treble crochet	Wrap yarn around hook, insert hook into st or sp indicated, yo, pull loop to front (3 loops on hook), 2x [yo, pull through 2 loops on hook].
	mtr	modified treble crochet	Wrap yarn around hook, insert hook in st or sp indicated, pull loop to front (3 loops on hook), yo, pull through 2 loops, insert your hook in the st behind from the previous round and pull a loop to the front and through both loops on the hook.
	hdtr	half double treble crochet	Wrap yarn around hook twice, insert hook into st or sp indicated, yo, pull loop to front (4 loops on hook), yo, pull through 2 loops (3 loops on hook), yo, pull through all 3 loops on hook.
	dtr	double treble crochet	Wrap yarn around hook twice, insert hook into st or sp indicated, yo, pull loop to front (4 loops on hook), 3x [yo, pull through 2 loops].

Techniques

	blo	back loop only	Insert hook into the back loop only of the st indicated.
	flo	front loop only	Insert hook into the front loop only of the st indicated.
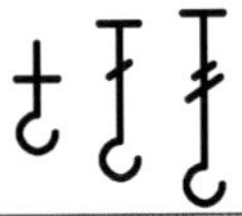	bp	back post	Insert hook around the post of the st indicated from the back.
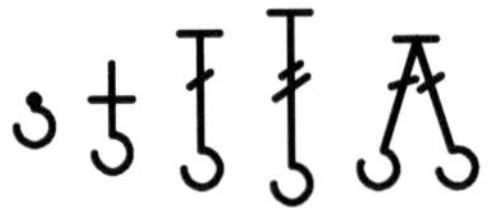	fp	front post	Insert hook around the post of the st indicated from the front.
	cl	cluster	Numerous sts worked together in the same st or sp. Could be any number of any kind of st, e.g. 3htrcl, 4trcl, 5dtrcl.
	inv join	invisible join	Cut yarn after completing last st of round. Pull tail up through the last st, thread tail onto needle, insert needle under "v" of first true st of the round and back through the centre of the last st, and through the lbv of the last st. Pull tight enough to form a "v" on top of the stch, weave end away.
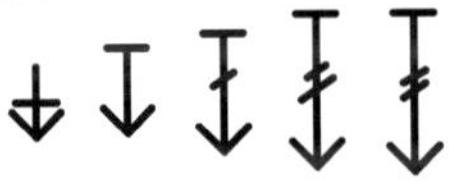	lbv	loop behind v	The third loop or back bump of a st on the back. It is located under the back loop of a st.
	mc	magic circle	Method used to begin a square. Wrap yarn around a few fingers, forming a loop, insert your hook into the centre and pull the working yarn through, ch1 to secure. Work R1 sts into the ring, pull the tail to close the ring once all sts have been made and secure by weaving the end in well.
	picot	picot stitch	ch3, ss into first ch.
	pcl	point cluster	First and last legs of tr3tog are fp, middle leg is worked into st.
	puff	puff stitch	Insert hook into st or sp indicated, 4x [yo, pull loop to front] (9 loops on hook), yo, pull through all loops on hook.
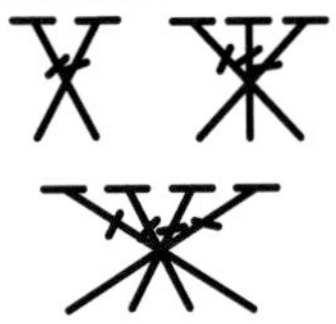	χ	skip cross stitch	2χ = skip 1 st, tr in next st, tr in skipped st. 3χ = skip 2 sts, tr in next st, tr in 2nd skipped st, tr in first skipped st. 4χ = skip 3 sts, tr in next st, tr in 3rd skipped st, tr in 2nd skipped st, tr in first skipped st.
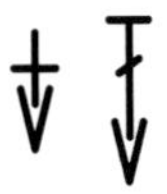	spike	spike st	Insert hook into st or sp indicated, usually in a round more than 1 round prior to the current round, pull up a long loop level with the current round and work st as normal. Can be any st, e.g. spike dc, spike tr.
	tog	together	Numerous sts worked together. Work the specified number of sts up to just before the last step, end with a yo and pull through all loops on hook. "tog" will be followed by "over next # sts". It can be done with different numbers and types of sts, e.g. dc2tog over next 2 sts , tr5tog over next 5 sts.

Yarn Information

This is where you will find the details of the yarn I used to make the all of the squares. Of course, you can use any yarn and hook combination you like.

Yarn Used Properties

Bendigo Woollen Mills 8 ply cotton

A: Sky

B: Blue Ice

C: Arctic

D: Parchment

22 sts / 10 cm (4"), 2.425 metres per gram

Pattern	Metres per colour per square				
	A	B	C	D	Single Colour
Aden	6	12.5	9	10.5	38
Adriatic	4	4.5	12.5	13.5	34.5
Aegean	2.5	6	8	15.5	32
Alboran	5	9	12	13.5	39.5
Andaman	7.5	7.5	15	12.5	42.5
Arafura	6	8.5	5	12.5	32
Azov	3.5	7	13	14	37.5
Baffin	7.5	13.5	12	7	40
Baltic	4	10	12	14	40
Banda	4	6.5	8.5	16	35
Beaufort	5	11.5	13	14	43.5
Bellinghausen	5.5	24	7.5	10.5	47.5
Bengal	2.5	8.5	13	24	48
Biscay	8.5	8.5	6	9.5	32.5
Bismarck	7	13	6	8.5	34.5
Bohai	5	9	9.5	24	47.5
Carribean	8	7	16	6.5	37.5
Carpentaria	5.5	7.5	10.5	14.5	38
Caspian	6.5	6.5	13.5	10.5	37
Catalan	6.5	17.5	10	7	41
Celebes	5.5	8	9	24.5	47
Ceram	4	6.5	8.5	15.5	34.5

Pattern	Metres per colour per square				
	A	B	C	D	Single Colour
Cooperation	6.5	7.5	9.5	17.5	41
Coral	4.5	6.5	11.5	10	32.5
Cortes	3	7	18.5	11.5	40
Drake	9	9	15	15.5	48.5
D'Urville	9	8.5	11	14	42.5
Flores	3	4	15.5	14.5	37
Hudson	6	9	15	8.5	38.5
Ionian	7	6	11	9.5	33.5
Java	5	10	12	6	33
Kara	4	7.5	10	13	34.5
Kattegat	4.5	7	10	16.5	38
Koro	8	8	6	11	33
Lazarev	6	7	11	11	35
Levantine	5.5	7	9	15	36.5
Maine	6.5	14.5	6	20	47
Marmara	6	8	7.5	18	39.5
Mawson	5	11	13	16	45
Molucca	8	7	14	12.5	41.5
Mozambique	4	9.5	13	11.5	38
Norwegian	11.5	9.5	12	6	39
Okhotsk	5.5	7	16	19.5	48
Oresund	3.5	7	14.5	12.5	37.5

Pattern	Metres per colour per square				
	A	**B**	**C**	**D**	**Single Colour**
Pacific	8.5	9	12	10	39.5
Pechora	6.5	15	7	11	39.5
Persian	10	10	6	10.5	36.5
Riga	6.5	8.5	6.5	14	35.5
Salish	4.5	7.5	11	14.5	37.5
Salton	6	11	9	17.5	43.5
Sardinia	6	11	17	6.5	40.5
Sargasso	5	5	14	14	38
Scotia	4	9.5	10	9.5	33
Seto	7.5	11	11.5	10.5	40.5
Sibuyan	7.5	13	7.5	11.5	39.5
Sicily	4	7	9	10.5	30.5
Sidra	4.5	5.5	11	20	41
Solomon	3	6.5	9	16	34.5
Somov	6.5	14	9	13.5	43
Sulu	8	11.5	16.5	6.5	42.5
Tasman	4	6	7	20	37
Thracian	6	10	6.5	18.5	41
Visayan	4.5	5.5	9	16.5	35.5
Weddell	7.5	7	10	19	43.5
Totals	**371**	**574**	**689**	**858**	**2491**

Acknowledgements

A second book! It would not have happened without the help of many folks and I am so grateful to my team for their awesome help.

Thanks, once again, Michelle Lorimer for your wonderful graphic design work. Thank you, Jo O'Keefe, for the super photography. Thanks to Kirsten Gittens for the author photo taken on my cruise to New Zealand in Milford Sound.

Thank you to the wonderful models, Josephine Fares, Julian Calcagnino, Sally Coffey, Baby Patrick, Leroy Kirk Walker, Tex O'Keefe and Scott Moore.

Thank you, SiewBee Pond, for your fabulous technical editing and proofreading. Thanks to Amy Gunderson, for making my patterns sing in chart form. They're so lovely on their own!

Thank you, Samantha Taylor, for making the Mini Sampler Blanket so beautifully for me.

My pattern testing team were troopers, getting all the patterns tested over and over. So much work for which I am forever grateful. Thank you, Anna, Bonita, Carmen, Chantelle, Donnisha, Hayley, Jeanette, Jennifer, Judy, Kathy, Keri-An, Lyn, Marion, Meghan, Melissa, Monica, Nicole H, Nikki, Ruth, Sam, Shona, Sharon B, Sharon L, Stephanie, Tammy R, Tammy T, Teresa, Tharana and Ursula.

Thank you to Bendigo Woollen Mills for supplying the yarn for me to make most of what you see in this book.

Thank you to all who supported the original release of the Siren's Atlas digital collection. That led me to be able to work on my first book, Granny Square Flair. Which leads me to my next thank you! And it is a big one to all the folks from all around the world who had such a fantastic reaction to Granny Square Flair. It has led to so many wonderful things like teaching all over Australia as well as on cruise ships! I have had a ball meeting so many of you and seeing all the amazing things you have made with my granny square patterns. I hope to see more of you in my future travels.

xx Shelley

About the Author

Shelley Husband is an Australian crochet designer and crochet teacher living on the south west coast of Victoria with her hubby and teenager in a tiny dot of a town by the ocean. Her two older children have left the nest and are spreading their own crafty and arty wings out in the world.

Shelley has crafted most of her life, trying "all of the crafts" over the years. These days, she spends most of her time with a crochet hook in hand. Having discovered a natural knack for crochet about seven years ago after a break of a few decades, she hasn't looked back, creating hundreds of Granny Square patterns.

Shelley loves nothing more than designing new patterns aiming to extend her own and our crochet skills, gently challenging and encouraging us to create timeless, classic pieces sure to be admired and appreciated.

Seamless crochet is a real passion and she has many tips and tricks to make our crochet look the best it possibly can, using techniques she has combined and tweaked over the years.

When not designing crochet, you can find Shelley teaching crochet in workshops around Victoria and beyond. For those who cannot make a workshop in person, she teaches worldwide via her annual Crochet-A-Long projects through her blog and YouTube channel. There is no doubting Shelley's passion for all things crochet.

You can find Shelley online at www.spincushions.com and on most social media channels as spincushions.

Find Shelley's other print books, **Granny Square Flair** and **Beneath the Surface Crochet Blanket** at your favourite online book retailer.

Find Shelley's ebooks on Amazon, iTunes and Kobo

* Granny Square Crochet for Beginners
* More than a Granny
* More than a Granny 2
* Flowers Abound
* Fran Crochet Blanket
* Greg Crochet Blanket
* Kaboom Crochet Blanket
* Mayan Crochet Blanket
* Granny Square Flair
* Beneath the Surface

Printed in Great Britain
by Amazon

28638369R00053